sales
compensation
made simple

Joseph DiMisa

About WorldatWork®

WorldatWork (www.worldatwork.org) is a global human resources association focused on compensation, benefits, work-life and integrated total rewards to attract, motivate and retain a talented workforce. Founded in 1955, WorldatWork provides a network of more than 30,000 members and professionals in 75 countries with training, certification, research, conferences and community. It has offices in Scottsdale, Arizona, and Washington, D.C.

ISBN: 978-1-57963-214-4 (Paperback/softback)
       978-1-57963-241-0 (E-book)

Editor: Andrea Ozias

Creative Services Manager: Rebecca Williams Ficker

Graphic Design: Hanna Norris

WorldatWork.
The Total Rewards Association

www.worldatwork.org

Table of Contents

Introduction

Years ago, before they were so complex, a sales organization might have had one flavor of sales representative — an account executive assigned to cover a defined territory, like the state of Tennessee. That sales representative likely had a "T2 Plan": "... the State of Tennessee and a 2-percent commission on everything you sell." Pretty straightforward.

In contrast, today's sales organizations are multifaceted and require multiple sales jobs with different responsibilities coupled with intricate forms of measurement and compensation. Accordingly, complex systems are required to help manage these complex organizations, and many companies struggle with the basic tenets of how to motivate and reward a sales organization.

The various components, process steps and "what if" assumptions can overwhelm experienced corporate executives, sales leaders, or sales or marketing professionals. What if you're not a compensation practitioner? Maybe you're a business professional who must understand sales compensation design. Or you may be a participant on a sales incentive design team providing expertise on your subject matter, but you're new to sales compensation. You need quick access to key questions to get up to speed so you can confidently participate in discussions, knowledgeably ask questions and bring insight to the plan design critique.

Truth be told, it doesn't need to be that hard to compensate a salesperson. If you understand the basics of an organization's business strategy and how an organization makes a profit, tying someone's compensation to this strategy is not a complicated process. Certainly you need to understand the steps, timing and overall process of how to build a plan, but if you remember the important organizational goals and ultimately align your rewards structure with the business strategy, you can design a plan that delivers sales results.

When I left the corporate world and moved into consulting, I eagerly anticipated gaining access to the Holy Grail of consulting: the "best practices closet," which I imagined would be filled with the tools to address every client issue and problem. But I never found that closet door. Instead, I gained opportunities to interact with a broad and diverse group of human resources professionals, clients and consultants from various firms, and participate in sales and compensation forums. From those interactions and my observations of how sales organizations do — and don't — work, I've been able to stock my own closet with a variety of concepts, process charts, graphics, probing questions and industry examples that help organizations make decisions about sales compensation. While perhaps not new to others, most of this information was new to me. The opportunity to have it in one place and in a concise manner provided me with a better understanding of how world-class compensation is developed.

In this book, I share what I've learned about the process and steps for developing an effective sales incentive compensation plan. I walk readers through tried-and-true approaches used for years by seasoned sales compensation consultants. Much of the thinking is informed by those early days of sales effectiveness consulting, when very simple terms, charts and graphs were created and effectively deployed to validate this new compensation area and grab the attention of sales executives and their corporate leaders.

Two of the most important concepts, which I consider to be "keepers," are the Growth Management System chart and the Optimal Sales Compensation Design Process chart. The ideas presented in these charts truly can charge up a sales organization and propel it toward powerful results. If you understand these two well-proven and unadulterated methodologies and their concepts, you can offer an authoritative perspective on sales compensation.

My goal in writing this book is to give you a foundation and help you fortify your knowledge with basic methods and graphics you can use to explain, develop and coach the people around you. For the experienced, these methods and ideas will no doubt be familiar — providing reinforcement of the process your organization employs. For those new to incentive design, you can have confidence that the best practices described in this book are just that: tried-and-true ways to approach the challenges and complexities of incentive design and bring logic and simplicity to your undertaking. Regardless of your experience level, I sincerely hope you enjoy the book and find it valuable in increasing your knowledge and building a strong base of intelligence that leads to effective sales compensation plans.

1 The Growth Management System and Optimal Sales Compensation Design Process

Sales compensation, or incentive pay, is a method or pay system that allows an organization to reward a salesperson for positive results. The system or method creates an output that typically is dollars paid to that person. Sales compensation enables management to align pay opportunity with the strategy and objectives of the business. If done correctly, compensation will help an organization attract, retain and motivate top salespeople. If done incorrectly, it can result in turnover issues, drive inappropriate behaviors and/or increase uncontrolled sales costs. This chapter explains why it's important to align sales compensation with the overall business and sales strategies, and the seven essential steps in the incentive design process.

A Simple Design Process to Get You Started

As you begin the sales compensation design journey, you and your design team must be able to answer this question: *What is the organization and/or salesforce trying to accomplish?* Sales compensation design that proceeds without a clear answer will fail. Think about it this way: A sales compensation plan is put in place to motivate and reward certain sales behavior. The behavior can range from selling more products ("any sale is a good sale") and retaining and renewing current contracts, to acquiring new customers.

Before designing a plan, you must know what the organization wants to achieve. Without that knowledge, it's like asking a tailor to make you a suit, but then leaving the shop before your measurements are taken. You can't create the end product without the right input first. Knowing the strategy is important because it:

- Helps you understand what the organization wants to do
- Provides a road map and helps you define success
- Allows you to tie pay to the achievement of success.

**Compensation Is Not a Substitute
for Effective Management**

Sales compensation may complement other forms of pay, but the distinguishing factor is that sales compensation recognizes and rewards the unique responsibilities of a salesperson's job. In no way, shape or form is compensation a proxy for managing sales professionals. Managers need to manage reps by teaching, motivating and driving behavior. Compensation then becomes the means to focus reps on the right goals and reward behavior that produces sales results.

'Keeper' Chart No. 1: The Growth Management System

Plug a vacuum, hair dryer, air conditioner and microwave into the same circuit and that circuit most likely will blow. You can run to the box and flip the switch to get everything working again, but those appliances will more than likely power on, then sputter out again within minutes. Flipping the breaker doesn't fix the problem; it provides a temporary resolution. To really solve the problem, you need to go to the source — the various appliances, one of which needs to be switched to another circuit.

What does this have to do with sales compensation? Plenty. You can change your compensation plans in pursuit of better results but, in the end, if compensation issues (e.g., "Am I getting paid enough?") are really caused by something else (e.g., are quotas too high?), fixing compensation is not going to help. The breaker will blow again.

Certain graphics can cause the proverbial light to go on, illuminating a concept and fostering understanding. My introduction to the Growth Management System, illustrated in Figure 1-1, brought an early epiphany. If you take only a few things away from this book, make this chart one of them.

The Growth Management System captures in one place the pathway or approach to integrating sales compensation with organization and sales strategy. High-performing sales organizations — those that consistently lead their industry in terms of revenue, operating

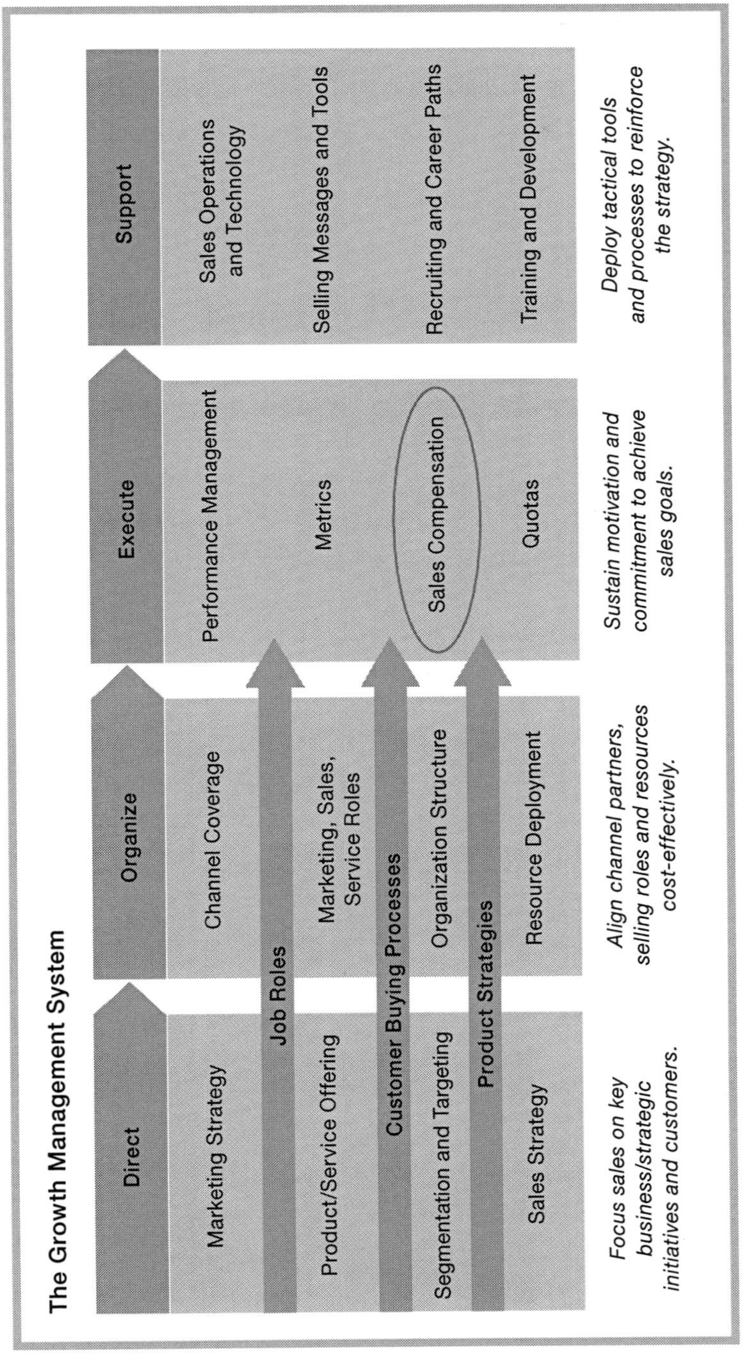

The Growth Management System

Direct	Organize	Execute	Support
Marketing Strategy	Channel Coverage	Performance Management	Sales Operations and Technology
Product/Service Offering	Marketing, Sales, Service Roles	Metrics	Selling Messages and Tools
Segmentation and Targeting	Organization Structure	Sales Compensation	Recruiting and Career Paths
Sales Strategy	Resource Deployment	Quotas	Training and Development
Focus sales on key business/strategic initiatives and customers.	*Align channel partners, selling roles and resources cost-effectively.*	*Sustain motivation and commitment to achieve sales goals.*	*Deploy tactical tools and processes to reinforce the strategy.*

Connecting arrows between Direct and Organize: Job Roles, Customer Buying Processes, Product Strategies

FIGURE 1-1

profit and total shareholder return — identify and successfully address their overall growth strategies. In doing so, they develop systematic approaches to sales that group and link all critical factors to four key groupings, which in turn govern the following four actions:

- **Direct:** The strategic course the company wants to take with its customers and products
- **Organize:** The way a company structures the organization to meet its directional goals
- **Execute:** The means by which an organization plans to tactically implement its organizational and directional goals (this is where compensation comes into play)
- **Support:** The tactics, technology and processes the organization deploys to equip itself to realize the strategy.

Figure 1-1 illustrates the key disciplines for all four groups. In all, 16 areas need to be addressed when managing a sales organization; any of these can cause a circuit malfunction within the sales organization.

The Growth Management System highlights how market factors and business strategy drive sales execution and incentive compensation. To build growth capability, successful sales organizations develop and align their ability to direct with a strategy, organize around target markets, execute to the objective and support the organization. Upstream strategic decisions and downstream tactics must align. Within the execute circuit, compensation is an important component that is built upon strategic elements and supported by other groups.

Pay Is Not Always the Problem

Organizations too often point to sales compensation as the source of or solution for a variety of problems. If an organization has high turnover or is not meeting sales objectives, it is easy to conclude that compensation is the culprit: "We need to pay people more to keep them," or "They won't sell more unless they're paid more."

You've likely heard these comments around a conference table. On the surface, pay seems like a logical place to start; in reality, it is the worst place to start. Remember: Compensation is how you motivate and reward. If reps are exiting in droves or seriously underperforming, paying them more might ease the problem for a while, but it wouldn't fix the problem because you haven't made the proper diagnosis. You need to look at all the disciplines that come before compensation to figure out the issue. To dive right into changing the compensation plan without understanding where the problem is or how other areas affect your compensation plan design can bring your system to a standstill — and even cause it to blow — if not today, then later down the road.

Several years ago, I was asked to fix the compensation plan of a company suffering from major turnover in the direct salesforce — more than 45 percent annually. Some unofficial exit interviews suggested that reps were disenchanted with their pay. They felt the value of their rewards was not commensurate with their sales efforts: "Tough job, low pay" was the refrain. The director wanted some benchmarking and a more profitable sales compensation design.

Following the Growth Management System, my team assessed all of the disciplines in the organization, not just the compensation plan. We also looked at exactly who was leaving and their tenure. Our conclusions: First, pay was not the issue. The true problem was misalignment of the sales channel with customers and products. Second, the job roles in those channels had to sell complex products, but the sales representatives lacked the experience and know-how to sell these products. As such, their pay and compensation plan was fine, but it was not paying out properly due to a misalignment of channels and job roles. Additionally, the turnover was occurring primarily with representatives who had less than two years of tenure. Reps who made it past two years typically stayed because they had built up sufficient skills to make their sales. If they could not gain those skills, they were being starved out (low pay) and leaving.

As we presented our findings, I could see the wheels starting to spin in the minds of the executive steering committee. It was not compensation, but the *strategy* that was causing the issues. We redesigned the channels and job roles and made only minor modifications to the compensation plans (with no change to target pay levels).

Keep It Current

As the business changes, so must sales programs and compensation plans. Companies typically move through several growth phases as they mature. In each phase, the company uses unique sales strategies, coverage approaches and sales compensation plans. If the organization does not recognize these changes in its market, competition and business environment, programs that previously were effective become ineffective, putting the company at a competitive disadvantage.

The Information You Need and Where to Find It

The Growth Management System raises some questions: Where do you get the sales effectiveness information identified in the chart? What resources are available to get a handle on the organization's strategies?

A good place to start may be with sales, sales operations, finance, marketing, HR and, in some instances, IT. These resources likely have the data you need and can access it fairly quickly. If you work for a smaller company and do not have the resources, then you may need to look at the business plan or query senior executives to get the information.

Seek out the following types of information:

- **High-level organizational strategies:** Are there any organizational influences, issues, points or information that may affect planning (e.g., additional hiring, mergers and acquisitions, anything out of the ordinary)?

- **Organization's overall plans to segment and target customers:** What is the organization selling? How much effort is needed to make the sales? How long is the selling process? The answers to these questions help determine appropriate pay mix or optimum length of payout cycles.

- **Sales channels:** Which channels are being used? Some are more valuable than others or have higher costs. This will help you match jobs with channels and understand why benchmark jobs in salary surveys may have higher or lower compensation levels.

- **Job roles that target customers:** What job roles are you benchmarking? What do they do? What experience is needed? What competencies are needed?

- **Overall revenue/product commitment:** What are the overall quota or product commitments (as opposed to individual quotas)?

Figure 1-2 provides a more detailed data request list.

'Keeper' Chart No. 2: The Optimal Sales Compensation Design Process

The Growth Management System focuses attention on the complete sales organization; the second "keeper" chart outlines and focuses on the components that come into play when designing sales incentives and measuring a plan's effectiveness. The Optimal Sales Compensation Design Process lays out the fundamental process for sales compensation design. As such, it establishes the foundation for all that follows. The Growth Management System shows that effective compensation evaluation and design is driven by an understanding of the organization's decisions on strategy and market coverage. The Optimal Sales Compensation Design Process takes that concept to the next level, illustrating the seven aspects to address when evaluating and designing sales compensation plans.

As shown in Figure 1-3, effective sales compensation or the optimal design process starts at the 12 o'clock position with "job roles" and moves clockwise, ultimately coming full cycle to the

FIGURE 1-2

Sample Data Request

General/Demographic Data

- Employee name
- Employee number
- Manager name
- Job title
- Assignment number
- Region/location
- Full- or part-time designation
- Compensation program
- Company start date
- Position start date
- Term date

Quantitative Data

- Year-to-date pay and performance data by incumbent for current year and at least the past year
- Year-to-date revenue and/or profit by customer/account (as available) for current year and at least the past year
- Organization and/or region-level performance data
- Sales forecast versus actual sales by company, business unit and product for current year and at least the past year
- Relevant performance reports that are regularly provided to the sales organization
- Headcount by role and location
- Turnover data
- Currency conversion rates used for revenue crediting and compensation

Qualitative Data

- Copy of current sales compensation plans, including all plan descriptions and performance criteria (current year and previous years, if different)
- Job profiles/data
- Company business plan document
- Field training documents
- Field presentations
- Marketing plans
- Recognition program documents
- Other contest/product rewards
- Other incentive program documentation
- Organization charts
- Exit interview information

Individual Pay and Performance Information (Annually)

- Base pay
- Actual sales performance for each performance measure in the sales incentive plan (e.g., volume, profit dollars, profit margin, profit growth)
- Actual incentive compensation attributable to each performance measure in the sales plan
- Sales performance goals for each performance measure in the sales plan
- Target incentive compensation based on performance goals for each performance measure in the sales plan
- Other incentives paid (e.g., any other rewards outside the incentive plan)

evaluation and next-cycle planning step. These seven steps create a simple yet potent process for sales compensation design. Once you understand these steps and the proper questions to ask the sales team or organization, you are well on your way to fashioning an effective design.

Every step has a role and is important to the process. It is important to stay focused on this process. Also, steps cannot be skipped, as they are sequential. Think about it: You can't get to 8 p.m. until you have moved through the morning and afternoon. It's the same thing with sales compensation. You can't start talking about the measures in a plan and the commission rates until you have determined whether the job is eligible and what the mix of base pay and incentive will be.

The balance of this book discusses each aspect of the process, explaining the methods compensation professionals use. Remember that all aspects of the optimum design process tie back to strategy;

FIGURE 1-3

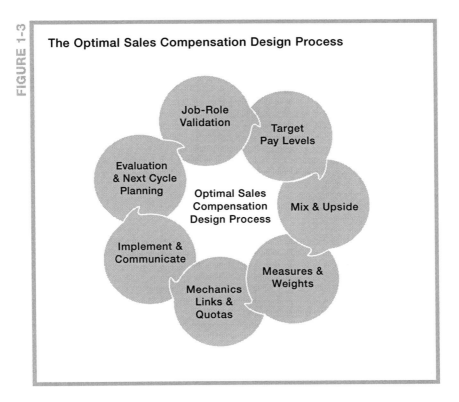

The Optimal Sales Compensation Design Process

Job-Role Validation

Target Pay Levels

Evaluation & Next Cycle Planning

Optimal Sales Compensation Design Process

Mix & Upside

Implement & Communicate

Measures & Weights

Mechanics Links & Quotas

if you don't know your strategy, stop right here. There's no point in taking any more steps if you haven't taken the critical first step.

Anyone who has been involved in sales compensation for any period of time likely has encountered the Growth Management System and Optimal Sales Compensation Incentive Design Process, or similar charts with different names. The source of a chart and its title don't matter — it's the concepts that count. The "keeper" concepts from these two charts are:

- Get a handle on how your organization directs, organizes, executes and supports strategy in the sales organization.

- Make sure any blips in sales performance truly are compensation-related before embarking on incentive redesign.

- When you set out to monitor a sales compensation plan or design a new approach, let the components of the optimal design process guide your effort.

2 Job-Role Validation

Different sales jobs have different priorities. Ultimately, a sales job's priorities affect the design of the sales incentive plan. When sales roles are clearly defined, the incentive plan can drive specific behaviors and results. Many organizations struggle with which roles to include in sales incentive plans versus management bonus plans — or whether a job should be eligible for incentives at all. This chapter explains:

- How sales channels (i.e., the means through which a company interacts with its customers and distributes its products and services to its buyers or potential buyers) figure into job-role definition

- Which aspects of a job's role (i.e., critical success factors, priorities and relationships within the sales organization including marketing and sales support) to consider in sales incentive design

- How to determine if a job should be eligible for sales compensation.

Job Roles Are the Foundation

The Optimal Sales Compensation Design Process on page 19 is a great tool for understanding the components and intricacies of sales compensation. As discussed, sales compensation design starts at the 12 o'clock position with the job roles that you plan to include in the sales incentive plan. Understanding the success factors, priorities and relationships of these jobs will get incentive design started on the right foot.

Job roles inform all aspects of incentive design, from eligibility to quota setting and every step in between. You must understand what a job does, how it does it and why it does it. If a job is not well defined or if you wonder why the organization wants to put, for example, an IT manager on sales incentives, it's your responsibility to challenge the organization and ask for a better description. If you don't "get" the job, you won't know how to pay it. There are three things to know from the start:

- Whether jobs are from a direct (company-owned) or indirect (company partners) channel
- What role the jobs play in the overall sales process
- If a job should be incentive-eligible.

Know the Channel

I once asked a sales manager to describe his company's sales compensation plan. It seemed a simple request, but getting to the answer prompted a circuitous exchange: "Which one," he asked, looking confused. A bit confused myself, I replied, "How many do you have?"

We went back and forth answering questions with questions without resolving much. That exchange helped me to realize that an organization may have many compensation plans for many different roles. In addition, with multiple sales channels and support functions, the simple compensation request can have multiple answers.

A sales channel may be either direct with the customer or prospect, or indirect through a partner or agent of the company. The incentive implications for a job can vary based upon the channel's role in the sales process.

Roles Found in Direct Channels

In a direct channel, roles are primarily direct "feet on the street" representatives, but they also may be call center representatives. Different roles will have different responsibilities. Some typical roles might include:

- **Geographic representative:** Focuses on a specific territory, region or geography. This role typically would be responsible for selling, servicing or interacting with accounts in this predefined geography.

- **Industry representative or customer specialist:** Typically focuses on a specific industry (e.g., telecommunications) or a group of customers (e.g., lawyers or doctors) that have specific and specialized needs. These representatives have expertise in this industry or with the customer.

- **Product representative:** Specializes in certain products or services and, consequently, has extensive expertise in those areas. If a customer has interest in a specific product, that account's representative may ask a product representative to meet with the customer to explain the intricacies and benefits of the product.

- **Account, global or strategic representative:** Works with a company's most important or strategic accounts, or those with the greatest potential. This role is similar to a geographic representative, but is assigned to one or more customers rather than a region or geography.

Roles Common to Indirect Channels

In an indirect channel, the sales representatives sell a company's products, but they are not employees of that company. Therefore, the method of compensation is different from company-owned channels. Roles in indirect channels may not do all aspects of the sales process. In many cases, they are paid for a specific aspect of performance, such as generating the sale. You may not be involved in designing incentives for indirect channels (indirect plans usually are designed by a channel expert), but understanding the whole sales picture provides a fuller understanding of the sales roles that will be eligible for the plan being designed. Typical roles in an indirect channel may include:

- **Traditional agent representative:** Dedicated to selling/representing a company's products and services. In most cases, this representative sells that company's products and services exclusively and does not handle any competing products. He/she receives a commission on what he/she sells and/or payment for services (e.g., interacting with customers and building relationships on the company's behalf).

- **Manufacturer's representative:** Sells/resells products from multiple manufacturers. One company's product is in the representative's portfolio along with other products from other companies. The representative receives a commission or payment based upon products sold.

- **Pure resale representative:** Resells a company's products and services on his/her own. The role is similar to a traditional or manufacturing representative, but in most cases this role will resell and possibly rebrand the product. These representatives make money by selling a product at a price higher than the purchase price.

- **Value-add reseller representative (VAR):** Very similar to a pure sales representative, but VARs will customize or add value to the product before selling it. A good example is Dell selling computers featuring the Intel chip.

Clear Job Roles Are Critical to an Effective Incentive Design

When sales roles are clearly designed according to their priorities and based upon specific channel goals, the compensation plan can drive specific behaviors and results. Job-role requirements basically are the job's definition. When job design and definition are fuzzy, the plan will reward success sometimes ... if you're lucky.

Understand How Jobs May Specialize

To further understand a job's role, examine its focus, success factors, priorities and relationships. As shown in Figure 2-1, a framework of five filters helps define a job and, ultimately, guide the design of the compensation plans.

Customer Segmentation and Targeting

Segmentation defines the types of customers/accounts to which the job sells. Customers may be defined by size, type, strategic importance, geography, etc. Different types of accounts require different skill sets and selling techniques. Understanding segmentation and strategy helps you focus on what each job is about (i.e., how hard the job is, how hard it is to find customers). You need to know what type of customers the role is targeting and the skill sets required to perform to expectations. There are some key questions that can help collect that information:

- What/who are the assigned customers/targets?
- Are leads provided or do they need to be generated?
- How many accounts are current (customers), target (potential customers) or dormant (customers who haven't purchased in a while)?
- How often do representatives call on each category of customers?

FIGURE 2-1

Job Specialization Framework

Sales jobs can be specialized in five ways:

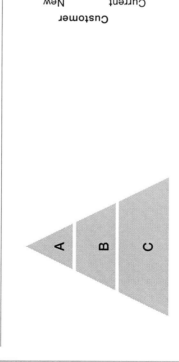

1. Segmentation

- Account segments typically are determined by size, customer type, strategic importance and/or other criteria.
- Varying account segments often require different skill sets and selling techniques/activities.

2. Sales Strategy

- Customer and product focus should support the sales strategy
- Primarily, sales strategy can focus on:
  - **Penetration:** acquiring greater sales with current customers
  - **Acquisition:** generating sales from new customers, either with new or current products
  - **Retention:** maintaining current sales with current customers.

FIGURE 2-1

Job Specialization Framework (Continued)

Sales jobs can be specialized in five ways:

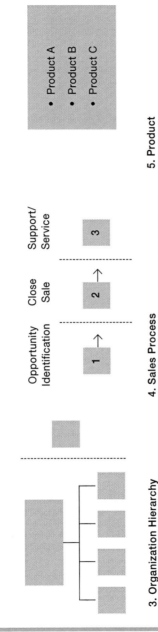

Opportunity Identification → Close Sale → Support/Service

- Product A
- Product B
- Product C

3. Organization Hierarchy

- Identify organizational and reporting structure (individual contributor versus manager, etc.)
- An account manager oversees all sales activity into an account and is supported by a team of sales representatives.
- In other cases, sales representatives independently cover an account; usually used for smaller, nonstrategic accounts.

4. Sales Process

- Identify specific steps within the sales process
- A focus on each process step requires different sales skills and mentality.

5. Product

- Identify the product and/or product lines
- Sales representatives develop in-depth technical knowledge and expertise in selling assigned products and/or product lines to many customers.

- Within the customer organization, who is the targeted purchaser?
- What is the representative's focus (e.g., major accounts, geography, etc.)?
- On what basis do customers make buying decisions (e.g., budget, opportunity for customization, etc.)?

Sales Strategy

Once the job's targeted customers are identified, you need to understand the job's primary sales strategy. Does the job need to find new customers? Sell more to existing customers? Maintain the revenue in existing accounts? Sales jobs have three primary stages, commonly referred to as PAR strategy:

- **Penetration:** acquiring greater sales with current customers
- **Acquisition:** generating sales from new customers, either through the sale of new or current products
- **Retention:** maintaining current sales with current customers.

Sales strategy helps determine the focus of the job, rather than the ease of the job. Each of the PAR strategies takes a different skill. Acquisition representatives are hunting for new customers; they have to create awareness and stimulate interest. When retention is the focus, the customer already knows the sales representative and the product, so the representative's role is to maintain the relationship. Penetration also involves relationship building but, in addition, the representative seeks new sources with current customers' organizations. Penetration involves crossing boundaries and broadening one's reach within an organization.

PAR strategies play a large role in how sales jobs should be compensated and, depending on the role, pay may differ significantly. Acquisition usually is considered the toughest — and most valuable — role. Penetration typically is second in importance and difficulty. Retention is about holding onto the base. It's often the most cost-effective and streamlined sale.

Questions related to the sales strategy include:

- What type of selling does this role do?
- How does this selling support the overall organizational strategy?
- How does the company value the different types of PAR revenue?
- How should the company compensate differently based upon the different roles and strategy?

Organization Hierarchy

The organization-hierarchy filter considers the supporting structure around the sales representative (e.g., do the representatives get help from others or are they on their own?). Sales jobs can be specialized by organization and reporting structure (e.g., individual contributor versus manager). An account manager oversees all sales activity into an account and is supported by a team of sales representatives. In other cases, sales representatives independently cover an account, most typically smaller, nonstrategic accounts. Questions that are important to the organization hierarchy include those that focus on the representative, as well as other roles that support the sales organization. The issue becomes whether these roles merit incentives, too.

- What resources within the company (human and other) does the seller use or have available throughout the selling process?
- What other support roles should be considered for incentive pay?
- How are the resources allocated/assigned?
- How is the sales manager involved in the transaction/selling process?

These questions cover the basic areas to explore. But keep in mind that, given the complexity of the sales organization and strategy, it might be relevant to also consider other external, noncustomer personnel who are involved in a transaction (e.g., resellers, distributors, marketing partners, fulfillment houses, etc.). Bottom line: The more complex your organization, the deeper you need to dig to flesh out the requirements, skills and demands of a sales job.

Sales Process

Sales process focuses on the steps a representative takes to complete the transaction — what is he/she actually doing? Does he/she identify, qualify, propose, close, fulfill? (See "The Five Steps in the Sales Process" for further explanation of the sales process.) Each step in the sales process has a value associated with it, and you need to understand that value. Generally, if a representative is identifying and qualifying only, pay may be lower. Representatives who propose or close might get more, but only to a point. Representatives who do it all likely will have higher pay. However, much depends on the type of industry and the way the salesforce is organized.

For example, a successful professional services firm needs people who can generate leads, provide the subject-matter expertise necessary to close the sale, and deliver the work. All of these activities are critical, but a firm may place a premium on individuals who can stimulate an opportunity and get the phone to ring. A car dealership, on the other hand, will value the closer.

The Five Steps in the Sales Process

A sales process typically includes the following five steps. How a company values each step and the sales job's role in each step influences not only eligibility for incentives, but also target pay, mix and upside, measures, mechanics and quotas.

1. **Identify** potential customers and why they might want the products or services. This step is about targeting prospects.

2. **Qualify** identified customers. Determine if they need the product or service and if that need is worth pursuing.

3. **Propose** the solution to qualified customers, either through a written proposal or in a meeting, explaining how the product or service will help the customer. Reaching the proposal stage increases the odds of making the sale.

4. **Close** the sale by negotiating the final details and terms. This is the confirmation step.

5. **Fulfill** the commitment to the customer and continue to add value as the company delivers its solution. Typically, representatives stay involved at a high level to ensure customer needs are met. If this step is botched, so is any hope for future sales.

Questions to ask about the overall sales process include:

- What are the steps the seller uses to complete the transaction (sales process)?
- Does the typical transaction cross all of these steps?
- Is a certain transaction more valuable than another?
- Is the transaction a one-time exchange or an ongoing flow of business?
- What is the length of the sales cycle?
- What is the amount of the sale for the various roles?
- What is the length of time within each process step? How long does it take to complete a sale from the initial lead? For example, if it takes a day to identify, a day to qualify, a day to propose and a day to close, the entire sales cycle is four days.
- How many transactions can occur within a payment cycle (e.g., monthly, quarterly, annually) for each customer?
- When is the transaction considered closed or complete (at order, at billing or at delivery/installation)?

Product

Sales jobs can be specialized according to product and/or product lines. Knowing a company's products helps you understand the job role, length of sales cycle and so on. Product is particularly important if representatives are specialized by product. Each product has an associated value, and you want to ensure the sales incentive is commensurate with a product's value and profit. Additionally, if representatives specialize in selling certain products (e.g., data, services and software specialists), they develop in-depth technical knowledge and expertise in selling assigned products and/or product lines to many customers. That expertise may be worth a premium.

Questions related to products and services include:

- What is the range of products or services the reseller represents?
- Do products/services differ by customer?
- Are the products sold "as is," or do they have to be customized for customer needs?

- How is each type of product or service measured in sales results (i.e., units, sales value, revenue, margin dollars, margin percent)?
- Are individual quotas set for the products or services?

Determine Eligibility

Once you understand what a job entails, you can do a sanity check to ensure it should be eligible for sales incentives. Many organizations struggle with this. Too often, emotion takes the place of pragmatism, and organizations add jobs to their sales incentive plans. Some decisions are well-founded; some are misguided. The right tool can take the emotion out of the decision and help determine whether incentives are appropriate for a given role.

Consider customer support roles as an example. As organizations become more customer-focused and performance-based, more support roles are created to help a customer and/or support a sales representative. Should a company reward that role through incentives? The decision depends on whether those roles truly influence the sale. Everyone likes the idea of earning incentive pay, but fewer are willing to take the trade-off between fixed and variable pay. Failing to balance variable and fixed pay appropriately may create a much higher cost of sales. (See Chapter 8 for more discussion.) In consulting, this issue is called "sales job role creep." Jobs that are in this questionable category include customer service roles, marketing roles, product marketing roles, technical support roles and some business development roles. Some of these roles fit the top-line definition of speaking to a customer and influencing a sale, but many do not.

The Job Profile Quiz can help determine eligibility for various jobs. Accurately answering the questions helps take the emotion out of the equation and pinpoint those jobs that truly deserve incentive pay because of what they do and how they do it. There are no right or wrong answers; every question requires thoughtful discussion and judgment. Based on the responses, a profile should emerge of a job's focus, demands and priorities.

Those jobs that skew toward greater complexity, more accountability and significant influence over customers and the sale are
likely the better candidates for incentive pay.

Job Profile Quiz

Current Function:_____

Job Title: _____

1.   How much of the job's time is spent in direct customer contact?

    a.   0%

    b.   1%-15%

    c.   16%-30%

    d.   31%-45%

    e.   >45%

2.   How are the accounts assigned?

    a.   Pooled

    b.   Geographic territory

    c.   Named accounts

    d.   Single account

3.   How much influence does the job have on the customer's buying decision?

    a.   Strong control

    b.   Primary influence

    c.   Moderate influence

    d.   Minimal influence

    e.   No influence

4.   How important is customer retention as a component of the job?

    a.   Primary (No. 1 job priority)

    b.   Secondary (No. 2 job priority)

    c.   Tertiary (No. 3 job priority)

    d.   Not important

5.   How important is upselling to customers as a component of the job?

    a.   Primary (No. 1 job priority)

    b.   Secondary (No. 2 job priority)

    c.   Tertiary (No. 3 job priority)

    d.   Not important

Job Profile Quiz (Continued)

6. How important is acquisition of new accounts as a component of the job?

   a.   Primary (No. 1 job priority)

   b.   Secondary (No. 2 job priority)

   c.   Tertiary (No. 3 job priority)

   d.   Not important

7. How is most of the job's time focused during the sales process?

   a.   Mostly precontract

   b.   Mostly post-contract

   c.   Neither

8. How important is product positioning and building a name brand as a component of the job?

   a.   None

   b.   Small

   c.   Primary

   d.   Secondary

9. How long is the average sales cycle for the customers?

   a.   18 months

   b.   12-18 months

   c.   6-12 months

   d.   3-6 months

   e.   <3 months

10. How measurable are the job-driven results?

   a.   Not measurable

   b.   Somewhat indirectly measurable

   c.   Indirectly measurable

   d.   Somewhat directly measurable

   e.   Directly measurable

3 Target Pay Levels

One of the most emotional areas of incentive design involves properly setting target pay levels. Get it right and the sales team feels good about the direction and opportunity; get it wrong and it will be raked over the coals in conference room discussions, hallway chatter and watercooler laments. To set target pay levels, you need a clear compensation philosophy that includes a pay positioning statement (i.e., where the company wants to pay against market: at, above, below), good market data on benchmark jobs and a pay structure based on competitive data. This chapter discusses:

- Which components are part of sales pay
- Why and how to establish a compensation philosophy and pay positioning policy
- How to assess survey data to set target pay levels for benchmark jobs
- How to structure pay bands.

Fixed and Variable Pay Components

Equipped with an understanding of both the organization's strategy and the job roles eligible for incentive pay, the next step is to determine the appropriate target pay levels for the various positions. In sales, most positions earn two types of pay:

- Base salary is a fixed amount of pay that is earned for fulfilling basic accountabilities and meeting performance expectations, such as performing quality work, being a team player, understanding the company's products or services, demonstrating job-specific competencies, etc.

- Incentive pay is earned for achieving predetermined goals, sales quotas and/or specific sales-related activities. Incentive pay, which may also be called a bonus or commission in some plans, increases as a representative continues to perform. Typically, incentives kick in when results reach a threshold level of performance; incentive earnings increase as results meet and exceed the goal or quota. At quota, the representative earns the target level of incentive; beyond quota, earnings typically exceed target pay levels. Incentive earnings may be less than target if performance is below quota.

Together, these components constitute a sales position's total target cash (TTC) compensation, also known as total cash compensation.

> **Total Target Cash (TTC)**
>
> TTC is the sum of all cash received for the job including base salary, commission and/or bonus. TTC excludes benefits or any other payments, such as car allowances or any special incentives or awards.

The term "target incentive" means that, at the target level of performance (typically 100 percent of goal or quota), a job earns the target level of pay. As shown in Figure 3-1, the position has the potential to earn target TTC of $100,000. Of that amount, $50,000 is salary and will be paid out according to the company payroll schedule. The other half must be earned as incentive pay and may be paid weekly, monthly or quarterly. In the example, the position has a $1 million quota. If the representative achieves that quota, then he/she earns the $50,000 target incentive. If the representative exceeds quota, he/she earns more than the target pay level. Below-quota performance results in a lower incentive or none at all.

The Importance of a Compensation Philosophy

Not long ago, I was helping a high-tech company review and reset its target pay levels. The market analysis showed that the company was paying above market for some positions and below market for others. "Which is right?" the client asked. I asked about the company's pay philosophy — the company's beliefs, principles or position on paying representatives. The client's response was vague. "We want to pay high enough so we don't lose our good people." That's not a lot to go on.

After continued discussions, the client saw the value of stating a well-defined policy regarding the company's preferred positioning against market (i.e., at, above or below the competitive market) and, if above or below, by how much. After vetting different

FIGURE 3-1

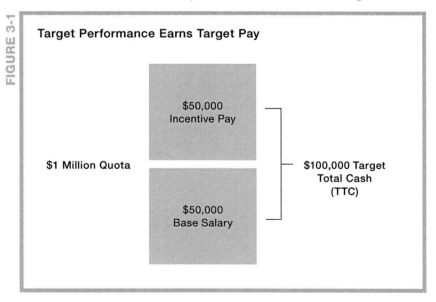

Target Performance Earns Target Pay

$1 Million Quota

$50,000 Incentive Pay

$50,000 Base Salary

$100,000 Target Total Cash (TTC)

options, it settled on the following principle: "Our company will consistently pay at the 65th percentile of the market as determined by at least three recognized market pay surveys."

A compensation philosophy establishes a set of guiding principles about what is important to the company and its position on pay. The philosophy becomes the reference point to steer and resolve debates over how to proceed. Establishing a compensation philosophy that specifically defines the company's approach to pay, especially pay positioning against the market, takes the guesswork and emotion out of pay analysis. As important, a compensation philosophy safeguards decision-making against the possible bias of one or more vocal sales managers or design team members.

In a recent compensation project, a large telecommunications company couldn't decide on the rate of pay for a particular account management job and how the role matched up against other roles. This type of indecision often occurs when new people join the pay design process or when decisions get difficult or emotions run high as management starts weighing in on a proposed course of action.

To help corral the group and manage the debate, we pulled out the company's compensation philosophy and read the pay positioning statement, which clearly stated the goal: "Pay above market levels (60th to 65th percentile) to help attract and retain top performers, while reducing pay of lower performers to help fund the payments." Once we read this statement and explained the relationships with pay and performance, there was less room for debate.

Companies that clearly articulate their overall position and the compensation goals they want to achieve face an easier design task, especially with the target pay discussion. As my first boss used to say, "Everyone has a strong opinion on how much we should pay." If you've put a philosophy stake in the ground beforehand, you have a strong foundation to support design activities. Figure 3-2 lists some principles that should be addressed in a pay philosophy. The Appendix includes a more complete list of principles and a statement of philosophy for each.

Pay Positioning

While all principles of a compensation philosophy are important, a company's pay positioning policy has a direct effect on how pay is delivered and what a sales representative can earn for achieving quota. As discussed, pay positioning defines where a company wants to pay relative to the market. Many companies pay at the median or 50th percentile — right in the middle of the competitive market. High-performing companies may want to pay at the 75th percentile, or even the 90th percentile, while others prefer a lower profile and set pay below competitive levels.

FIGURE 3-2

Principles of a Pay Philosophy

Role of pay	The role of pay in the overall employee value proposition, including the financial and nonfinancial rewards, and in driving desired performance results and behaviors.
Performance criteria	The performance categories that are reinforced through compensation. Categories typically vary based on the nature of employee and organization segmentation. The strategies for linking pay/performance to contribution.
Internal/external value	The basis for valuing work and jobs. Define the emphasis of internal versus external factors in the valuation process
Competitive positioning	The level of compensation delivered relative to the peer companies in the organization's competitive framework. The degree to which different competitive markets are needed for different employee segments.
Mix of pay	The desired mix and relative prominence of fixed (base salary) and variable (incentive) compensation.
Governance and decision making	Clearly defined roles, responsibilities and decision rights for the design, approval and management of compensation programs. The way in which overall compensation levels are managed to a budget.
Communication	The degree to which the compensation strategy, programs and processes are communicated.

Pay and Performance Alignment

Companies often will say they pay at the 75th percentile ... but look at their quotas. Do they represent 75th-percentile results? If quotas are set at 75th-percentile levels, representatives must perform at that rate to actually earn that rate. The reverse holds true as well. Companies with a stable, tenured workforce more than likely will set pay targets at a lower level, maybe the 40th percentile. They can afford this lower positioning against the market because, historically, their sales staff turnover has been low. Sales representatives are comfortable with the internal pay equity, and market comparison has not been an issue. Company strategy is to build a culture of winners and generate the feeling that "everyone here is a top performer who always makes quota." Companies with this strategy may set quotas lower, most likely at the 40th percentile, and many representatives meet or exceed quota. Given performance levels, these companies actually end up paying closer to the market rate, or the 50th percentile.

Factors that Influence Target Pay

Seven factors come into play when determining pay positioning. Focusing on these factors helps take the emotion out of the conversation and forces the design team to answer specific questions and then determine the pay positioning that matches the answers.

1. **Degree of company stability.** How solid is the company? Typically, startup companies have to pay more to attract top talent due to the risk implicit in a new venture. The more risk, the more reward is expected. More stable companies, or those with longevity and a proven business case or track record, may have less risk. Stability offers value, which is reflected in the total rewards strategy, allowing the company to consider lower targets.

2. **Desired business results.** How likely is the organization to meet its business goals? Easily attainable goals make a case for setting target pay at median or below. Companies with

tougher performance goals are more likely to pay much more for those results when achieved.

3. **Expected employee performance.** What is the sales representative's performance level? As with the previous factor, the tougher the goal, the higher the opportunity.

4. **Productivity level.** How productive is the organization? This primarily refers to margins or profit. If the company is profitable and sells services or products that generate a lot of profit, then it probably can (and will) pay for higher targets.

5. **Talent supply.** How abundant is the talent required for the job? Is it hard to get talented people? If yes, higher targets may be necessary to attract and retain them.

6. **Employee mobility.** How stable is the salesforce? Is the staff a group of "hired guns" who frequently move from company to company chasing higher pay? Or are they stable, loyal and likely to stick it out for the long term? The answer will significantly affect target positioning.

7. **Staffing.** What is the typical workload for sales representatives? Do they work in teams? Many people performing the same job can lessen the workload on one individual or group. Similarly, working in teams spreads accountability, possibly giving each individual less influence over a sale. In such cases, target pay may be set lower. Conversely, in a very lean organization, the workload may be greater, thus requiring higher targets for greater effort and responsibility.

Figure 3-3 provides a scale of possible responses to the question each factor poses. Responses on the left side of the scale suggest that low to median pay positioning may be appropriate; responses on the right may make a case for higher positioning. The factors should be considered in their entirety, with greater weight given to those factors that the company considers most important.

Market Pay Data

When setting target pay levels, an important input is the competitive pay data provided by reliable surveys and industry reports. Surveys provide competitive intelligence on the going rates in the market. They report an array of pay information for benchmark positions (i.e., the positions commonly found in most companies, such as sales representative, account executive, district manager, etc.). The process of matching one's job to those in the survey and obtaining competitive pay data often is called benchmarking or market pricing. It ensures that the company is aware of the external market and uses it as one input in setting pay levels.

Benchmarking should occur at least every two years, if not annually, to stay current on market changes. Effective benchmarking requires good data from a reputable source. (See "Survey Sources.")

FIGURE 3-3

Factors to Consider When Setting Target Pay

	Lower Targets		Higher Targets	
1. Degree of industry stability	Rock solid	High	Moderate	Low (shake-out)
2. Desired business results	Very likely	Probable	Difficult	Unlikely
3. Expected employee performance (at target)	Low	Average	Stretch	Exceptionally high
4. Productivity level	Low	Average	Above average	Very high
5. Talent supply	Abundant	Adequate	Limited	Scarce
6. Employee mobility	Low	Modest	Some hiring away by competitors	Frequent hiring away by competitors
7. Staffing	Excessive	Adequate	Light	Extremely lean
	40th	50th	60th	75th
		Percentile		

Survey Sources

Typical sources of competitive pay data include:

- **Published surveys.** These typically are conducted and published by professional organizations (e.g., industry associations or consulting firms). Some surveys are available only to participants, while others can be purchased (participants typically receive a substantial discount).

- **Customized surveys.** These surveys typically are commissioned for a specific purpose or are a highly customized cut of a published survey. The price varies by survey scope, type of analysis and overall sophistication of the final product.

- **Trade associations.** Specialized associations or groups of similar organizations will gather data that is made available to members. The data usually is very good, and comes directly from and is managed by members.

- **Professional recruiters.** Employment recruiters are great sources of information for hard-to-find jobs and/or organizations for which data may be hard to find. However, the data likely has not been vetted, so it may be suspect. This data may be used to confirm other sources, but should not be a sole source.

Issues to consider when deciding on benchmarking sources include:

- **Availability of published survey data.** Select surveys from reputable associations or consultants.

- **Cost.** Surveys are expensive, but discounts usually are available for participants.

- **Data age.** Most surveys are conducted annually or biennially. The fresher the data, the better. If you plan to age the data (to bring data from all sources to a common date), use an industry standard for the year(s). If a survey is too old, the data will be suspect even if aged.

- **Data reliability and validity.** The survey source should have a history of reliability and include appropriate participants (e.g., the right industries, both business and people competitors; companies of comparable size/reputation; etc.) and a sufficient number of participants. The better the group of participants, the better the data.

- **Types of jobs.** Job matches must be "apples to apples." If a survey description significantly differs from the benchmark position, consider adjusting the data (plus or minus) to account for the difference in job scope. A 10-percent adjustment is typical; if more than 20 percent is necessary, it's probably a bad match.

- **Ease of use.** Look for surveys that provide data by percentile and scope (e.g., company size), and use a clear methodology. You might have to defend your market analysis, so make sure you can document and defend your choice.

Surveys may provide sales pay data as actual compensation paid as well as target compensation. When reviewing data, be sure to compare actual earnings to actual competitor compensation, and compare targets to competitor targets. Comparing actual data to targets can give a wrong impression about competitiveness.

Even with data from reliable sources, however, benchmarking is part art and part science — all overlaid with significant emotion. You will never fully understand the dimensions of all the emotions that come into play. As such, it is critical to debate the strategy, not the emotion. A good rule is to obtain as much survey data as possible, show examples and identify all findings and approaches. And always link the discussion and decisions back to the business strategy, job roles and compensation philosophy.

A few years ago, I was ramping up a new consultant who had a great background: an Ivy League education and top project management skills. What this consultant lacked, though, was experience and a good understanding of how some of the sales compensation practices come into play in real life.

We were setting pay levels for a large pharmaceutical company. On the surface, matching the company's jobs to those in the survey seemed easy but, as we got into the data, it became apparent that survey pay levels were all over the board. The novice consultant questioned why this could occur since we had four top survey sources.

Benchmarking does not always deliver a clear answer. You have to go back to the corporate strategy and pay philosophy. A firm in constant hiring mode is trying to attract talent all the time. It needs a compelling story for potential recruits, so it sets target pay at the 75th percentile of the market or higher. Other companies with more stable workforces have lower turnover, so those companies can set targets at just below the 50th percentile. Similar companies, different philosophies.

Pay Banding

Jobs typically are grouped into levels, grades or bands. Each band has an associated pay range. The range defines the pay opportunities available to each job assigned to that band. Within the band, a company can pay incumbents differently based on a variety of factors, including experience, performance and/or geography. Pay bands typically represent base pay, but they may be based on incentive targets or total compensation.

Most bands have three anchor points: the midpoint, the minimum and the maximum. The midpoint reflects the market rate based on the company's pay positioning (e.g., market median). The band's pay range from minimum to maximum varies, but typically the minimum of the range is 20 percent less than the midpoint or target pay, and the maximum is 20 percent higher than the midpoint. In a vertical hierarchy of bands, the pay ranges usually overlap by about 10 percent to 15 percent on each end of the band. The low end of the band usually represents the 25th percentile; the high end of the band typically is the 75th percentile.

Target Pay Needs a Firm Rationale

Clearly, setting target pay levels is not an exact science. The more thought, input and vetting that is done to determine the best levels for a firm, the better. Documenting decision making and aligning it to a compensation philosophy helps establish a firm foundation not just for target pay, but for the other aspects of incentive design — mix and upside, measures and weights, mechanics, links and quotas. In the following chapters, it will become clear how a compensation philosophy becomes the springboard for almost all aspects of effective sales incentive design.

4 Mix and Upside

Mix is one of the three major issues that preoccupy plan designers (the other two are overall pay and measures). Clients ask:

- "Should mix be 60/40 or 55/45?"
- "How do we get the exact balance to psychologically drive behaviors?"
- "Do I want to pay more salary or put extra earnings at risk?"
- "Is an $80,000 salary with a $20,000 incentive motivational enough?"

Striking the right balance between fixed and variable pay components is critical to creating the motivational effect that will drive salespeople to perform. This balance allows the organization to ignite its top performers while continuing to motivate the average performers. This chapter explores:

- How mix, upside and excellence connect and interact

- How to establish a pay mix that fits the various job roles, product sales cycles and the sales process
- How to ensure the upside of incentive pay is meaningful and appropriate
- The necessary excellence point to motivate top performers to keep performing.

Pay Mix

"What is the appropriate mix for a job?" Clients often expect a quick and efficient answer. Yet questions about pay mix are not so easily answered and, in some cases, the solution can be complex. When people ask about mix, they want to know how to determine the ratio or split between base salary (fixed pay) and target incentive (variable pay); in other words, the mix between the two.

Taken together, base salary and the target incentive form total target cash (TTC) compensation. Mix is the split of TTC between base pay and incentive pay. If a job has a 50/50 mix, then 50 percent of TTC is delivered in base pay and the job has a target incentive equal to 50 percent of TTC. If a job has a TTC of $100,000 and a 50/50 mix, the base would be $50,000 and the target incentive would be $50,000.

In sales compensation, pay mix is defined in one of two ways:

- **Target mix**: This is what you expect to pay out for performance at quota or target (e.g., the $50,000 target in the aforementioned example).

- **Actual mix**: This is the mix paid out based on results achieved. Although a team of representatives may have the same target mix, their actual mix likely will differ at year end. So, if the job has a 50-percent target incentive, some representatives may earn the target amount. Others will earn more, and others will earn less. For example, if a representative performs above quota and earns total pay of $110,000 at the end of the year, the representative's actual pay is $50,000 salary and $60,000 incentive — an actual mix of 45/55.

How Mix, Upside and Excellence Connect and Interact

Although mix is a relatively simple concept, it can be one of the most misunderstood areas of pay. Clients often misidentify target mix, upside and excellence levels and express confusion about how these three concepts tie together. Other areas of misunderstanding include fixed mix plans, target mix plans and how merit increases and other changes in salary affect actual mix. Figure 4-1 provides terms and simple definitions.

Setting the right target mix helps balance a representative's target earnings to ensure he/she is properly motivated. Typically, pay mix is more aggressive (i.e., more pay is put at risk) when the sales role is more prominent in the sales process or has more influence over the sales results. For example, a mix with more than 40 percent of the TTC in incentive pay typically is considered more aggressive. Of course, "aggressive" is all in the eyes of the beholder, and a mix of 60/40 or 50/50 is becoming more common.

Target Mix Plan

A sales job needs a target to keep it in balance with other jobs and its role requirements. In most plans, a job's actual pay mix differs from the target mix. Actual mix varies as incentive is earned (or not earned) or as base pay changes. A target mix plan typically is the most prevalent type of plan. The key is to understand that the actual mix always will vary based on a representative's actual earnings.

Fixed Mix Plan

A fixed mix plan is less common, but still found in many industries. Many organizations call this a bonus plan. In a fixed mix plan, a representative's incentive target is a percentage of the base salary rather than a percentage of TTC. For example, a job with a fixed mix plan that has a base of $60,000 and a 20-percent incentive target has an incentive target of $12,000. To determine the mix, the $60,000 base salary is divided by the $12,000 incentive, resulting in a mix of 67/33. The TTC for the job is $72,000 ($60,000 base plus $12,000 incentive).

FIGURE 4-1

Pay Mix Terminology

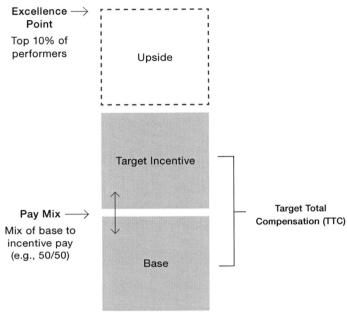

Excellence →
Point

Top 10% of
performers

Upside

Target Incentive

Pay Mix →

Mix of base to
incentive pay
(e.g., 50/50)

Base

Target Total
Compensation (TTC)

Base Salary: fixed portion of total target cash compensation that is used to distinguish differences in and reward for technical skill, selling skill, industry knowledge and experience

Excellence Point: achievement level that typically only the top 10 percent of sellers are expected to reach

Pay Mix: mix of base salary and target incentive; sometimes expressed as a percentage of base salary; typically, the more prominent the salesperson is in the sales process, the more pay is placed at risk

Performance Range: span of performance that earns incentive, extending from the specified minimum, or threshold, level of expected performance to the excellence point(s)

Target Incentive: amount of pay at risk for achieving sales targets

Total Target Cash (TTC) Compensation: base plus target incentive; also called "on-target earnings" (OTE) or "total cash compensation" (TCC)

Upside: amount of additional incentive pay that can be earned for achieving "outstanding" levels of performance

Sales compensation terminology can differ from industry to industry, from company to company. Figure 4-2 shows that very different terms may say the same thing or show compensation in different ways. But, at the end of the day, no matter how you express it, in each case the incentive target is $40,000 and the salary is $40,000. "Calculating Mix: A Quick Quiz" provides a few simple questions to test understanding of mix.

Mix by Job Role

Pay mix should vary for different jobs. A sales representative's prominence or involvement in the sale is a key factor in determining a job's mix. The more a representative "makes a sale happen," the more emphasis the incentive portion should receive. (See "Pay Mix Tips.") Other factors that influence a job's mix include:

- Market share
- Market size
- Customer acceptance of product
- Buying pattern
- Sales support
- Nonselling activities
- Team selling
- Risk taking
- Customer profile
- Job definition
- Control over the sales
- Control over the sales volume
- Close rate.

Figure 4-3 identifies situations that influence a job's mix.

When (if Ever) to Use a 0/100 Mix or 100-Percent Commission

A client once asked what I thought about paying commission only to a corporate salesforce. He liked the idea and had put his whole sales organization — a startup group of about 25 representatives within a larger technology firm — on 100-percent incentive with no base salary. His goal was to motivate his representatives to really hustle to generate new leads and opportunities, and acquire new business. He wanted his salesforce to always be "hungry." He believed this model would keep his fixed costs low because people would only be paid

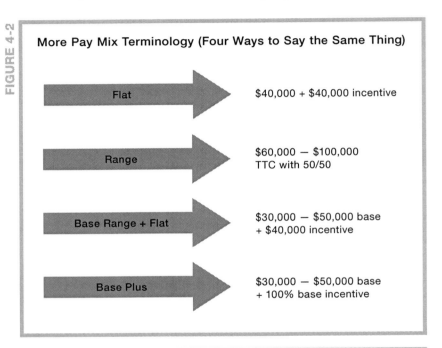

FIGURE 4-2

More Pay Mix Terminology (Four Ways to Say the Same Thing)

Flat → $40,000 + $40,000 incentive

Range → $60,000 — $100,000 TTC with 50/50

Base Range + Flat → $30,000 — $50,000 base + $40,000 incentive

Base Plus → $30,000 — $50,000 base + 100% base incentive

Calculating Mix: A Quick Quiz

Check your understanding of mix by answering the following questions.

1. If a representative has a TTC of $105,000 and a mix of 40/60, what is the base salary and the incentive target?

2. If a representative has a base salary of $68,000 and a target incentive of 25 percent of base, what is the mix and the target incentive?

3. If a representative has an incentive target of $44,000 and a mix of 70/30, what is the base salary and the TTC?

Answers:

1: $42,000 base salary, $63,000 target incentive.

2: 80/20 mix, $17,000 target incentive.

3: $102,667 base salary, $146,667 TTC

when they performed and the organization hit its targets. Pay was positioned well above market, and he was recruiting aggressive people. I responded to his question with a few questions of my own:

- How long had the business been operating under the current plan?

Pay Mix Tips

- Make sure both the amount of base salary and incentive are meaningful. If the incentive portion is insignificant, it may not be worth the representative's effort, or it may be viewed as a giveaway, so it will not motivate performance.

- Stay abreast of competitor/peer practices. Know what peers and competitors are paying and make sure you know why your company aligns with, or differs from, industry practices.

- Make sure the reward reflects the selling role. The level of representative effort needs to match the level of reward.

- Consider the sales cycle and number of transactions. The transactional nature of the job will dictate the level of representative involvement in a sale. For example, are they order takers and/or more transactional (more aggressive mix)? Or is the sales cycle long and time-consuming (less aggressive mix)?

FIGURE 4-3

Factors that Influence Pay Mix

More weight on base when:	More weight on incentives when:
• Selling is more of a team effort.	• The job requires a high level of skill and drive.
• There is heavy use of advertising and promotion.	• The company is not well-known.
• Product or service requires little sales effort.	• The product price is high versus the competition.
• Job includes many nonsales duties.	• Competition is strong.
• There is a longer sales cycle.	• Low advancement opportunities within the company.
• There is an emphasis on relationship management.	• Market opportunity is significant.

- How long are the representatives' sales cycles?
- What does overall TTC look like for the jobs?
- Do representatives get a draw (advanced payments) against future earnings?
- What's the targeted upside or leverage?
- What is the ramp-up time for someone becoming fully functioning?
- How stiff is the competition for talent?

It turned out that the plan had been in place for about six months, and the results were mixed. The overall sales cycle from qualification to close was about a month. TTC was slightly above market, while upside was well above. No draws were paid. No one had stayed in the job for more than five months, and it was tough attracting top talent. Clearly, such an aggressive mix was creating significant problems. The client hoped to build a tribe of hungry hunters, but he also was scaring people off by not providing appropriate cash flow and ramp-up time. With a competitive environment for sales talent, potential new hires were not willing to take such a risk.

Companies that want a very aggressive mix or one that is totally leveraged need to think about how representatives will get paid and how their cash flow looks. Aggressive can be workable, but it is important to understand the implications for hiring, retention, quality sales, customer service and representatives' cash flow. Companies that decide to go the 0/100 mix route need to provide appropriate ramp-up time for representatives to be fully functioning. It's a good idea to consider some advances on earnings to make up for the time between closing a sale and actual payment.

Upside Pay

"Upside" refers to the amount of additional incentive pay that can be earned for achieving outstanding levels of performance over the target incentive (i.e., above-target performance earns above-target incentive). Upside typically is expressed in ratio format.

A 1:1 ratio means that at target performance a sales representative can earn one times his/her target incentive. A 2:1 upside means earnings can be two times the target incentive.

Upside may be earned for any level of performance over the target up to a certain excellence point. At the excellence point, the representative tops out on earnings, reaches a cap or maximum, or continues to earn. Companies typically expect that only 10 percent or fewer representatives will reach the excellence point. A job with an aggressive mix typically needs a higher upside because the more risk sales representatives are given, the more reward they expect.

Upside is determined by the mix and incentive. If TTC is $100,000 with 20 percent of pay at risk and a 3:1 upside, then the representative can earn $60,000 in incentive. If the same job has a 50/50 mix, the representative can earn $50,000 in incentive and up to an additional $100,000 in upside.

Companies may establish upside on particular measures. For example, sales of Product A may have 4:1 upside; sales of Product B, 2:1; and sales of Product C, 3:1. Added together, overall leverage is 3:1 leverage.

Mix and upside work together. Figure 4-4 shows how setting mix may affect the total dollars that a representative can earn above excellence. Even though the upside is the same for similar jobs, dollars are significantly higher for representatives with a more aggressive mix. The more pay at risk, the more to be gained. Figure 4-5 shows typical mix and upside for benchmark jobs in a high-tech company.

Projected Earnings Distribution

When setting target mix and upside, it is important to estimate the aggregate earnings distribution of all representatives to the incentive plans. To accurately and prudently establish upside, project a representative distribution target for the organization. This means estimating how many representatives will perform below target, at target and above target. This distribution helps cost out the plan as well as finalize the excellence points and upside payout curves.

FIGURE 4-4

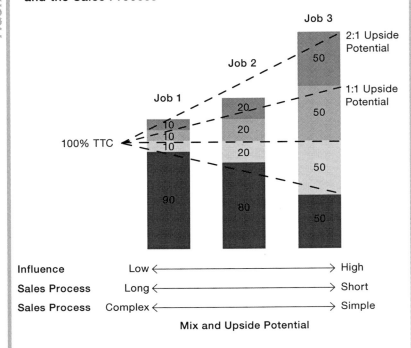

Mix and Upside Should Match Desired Behaviors and the Sales Process

Mix and Upside Potential

The three jobs shown here have the same TTC of $100,000, the same excellence points and the same upside potential.

- **Job 1** has a $90,000 base salary and $10,000 incentive target, or a 90/10 mix.

- **Job 2** has an 80/20 mix, or an $80,000 base salary and $20,000 incentive target.

- **Job 3** has a 50/50 mix, or a $50,000 base salary and $50,000 incentive target.

All positions share an upside ratio of 1:1 for the first excellence point and 2:1 for the second excellence point. Yet, the difference in earnings potential is dramatic:

- **Job 1**, at a 1:1 upside, earns one times target, or an additional $10,000. At two times target, it will earn $20,000 for a total potential incentive of $30,000. This is a 200-percent upside potential.

- **Job 2** has the potential to earn a total of $60,000 in incentives — again, a 200-percent upside.

- **Job 3** has the greatest opportunity (up to $150,000 in incentives at the second excellence point) — and the greatest risk.

Sample Mix and Upside Targets

Job Title	Typical Mix Range	Target Upside	Upside Impact
Territory Representative	40/60 – 60/40	2:1	220% or 180%
Account Manager	50/50 – 70/30	2:1	200% or 160%
Channel Manager	60/40 – 80/20	1.5:1	160% or 130%
District Manager	50/50 – 70/30	1.5:1	175% or 145%
Region Director	60/40 – 80/20	1:1	140% or 120%
System Engineer	75/25 – 85/15	1:1	125% or 115%
System Engineer Manager	80/20 – 85/15	1:1	120% or 115%

FIGURE 4-5

Figure 4-6 shows the desired distribution in a well-performing plan. As shown, 60 percent to 65 percent of representatives are at or above target. This means they will earn at least their target incentive and start earning upside or excellence pay. Roughly 5 percent to 10 percent of representatives perform at the excellence level and actually earn the highest upside pay. Conversely, 10 percent of the representatives fail to reach threshold (the minimum acceptable performance level). When setting target performance, planning for a bell-shaped distribution curve allows pay to be distributed accordingly and drives performance and accountability.

FIGURE 4-6

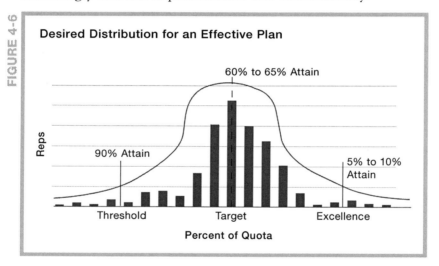

Desired Distribution for an Effective Plan

Test Your Knowledge

1. What is the mix of pay for a job with a $30,000 base salary and an incentive on two measures of $10,000 and $5,000?
   a. 50/50
   b. 65/35
   c. 75/25
   d. 80/20
2. What percentage of representatives should be at excellence level?
   a. 90 percent
   b. 30 percent
   c. 65 percent
   d. 10 percent
3. Pick two factors that help determine a higher mix of incentive versus base pay:
   a. Many nonsales functions
   b. More prominence in the sales process
   c. Significant market opportunity
   d. Team selling
4. If a representative has a $35,000 target incentive with an upside potential of 3:1, what total incentive pay can he/she receive at the top excellence point?
   a. $70,000
   b. $35,000
   c. $140,000
   d. $105,000
5. What type of role would have a 90/10 mix?
   a. Call center role
   b. New business representative
   c. Account representative
   d. Global account manager

Answers:
1. b
2. d
3. b and c
4. c
5. a

5 Measures and Weights

In today's complex selling world, many organizations struggle to decide which measures to use in their plan, how many measures to include and how much emphasis — or weight — to place on each measure. This chapter explains:

- General types of performance measures and when to use them

- How to determine the proper share of target incentive for each measure to ensure measures and weights drive sales reps' behavior.

At the kick-off meeting for one of my first sales compensation design projects, six corporate executives and four consultants were seated at a table in a large conference room. Sales, sales operations, HR, marketing, IT and finance all were represented.

To start the meeting, the sales operations leader, a rather vocal and dogmatic leader, allowed for some quick introductions and then jumped right into plan design, opining that the plan should have five measures: revenue, number of units, profit dollars, strategic product sales and overall division revenue. He also favored a subjective measure that allowed a sales manager to have some input on a representative's performance. Then he paused and asked if anyone had any issues with his approach. I noticed the concerned look on the face of my colleague, the consulting client manager. That troubled look was mirrored on the faces of each participant in the room — except, of course, on the face of our leader. For a kick-off design discussion, the cart was suddenly well ahead of the horse.

As I have gained experience through the years, I've seen this scenario repeated too many times. Compared to other aspects of incentive design, measures are concrete ... and maybe even sexy. People understand the cause and effect of measures; they appear to have the greatest effect on the success or failure of a sales compensation plan. Consequently, people want to jump into measures as the first step in the process when it's more appropriately the fourth step.

By rushing plan design, organizations run the risk of creating unbalanced plans that do not fully reflect the sales and business strategy and the sales roles. It's like selecting bait and tackle before you know what kind of fish you want to catch. You can end up motivating the wrong behavior, paying for the wrong results and diminishing the salesforce's motivation when the plan gets corrected midstream.

Performance Measures

The measures used in an incentive plan define the specific performance standards or criteria that determine success. Achievement against the measures becomes the basis for assessing sales results and awarding incentive payments. Generally, there are four types of measures (see Figure 5-1):

- Financial/production measures
- Strategic measures

Performance Measure Hierarchy

No more than three measures; no one measure less than 20 percent of target incentive.

Financial/Production Measures:

- Total net revenue
- Percent to goal

Strategic Measures:

- Product mix
- Customer mix
- Retention

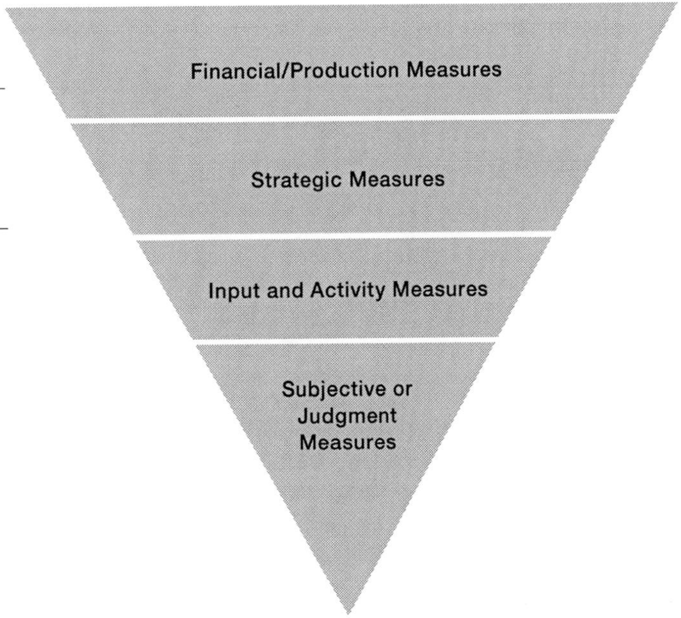

Input and Activity Measures:

- Activity measures (e.g., number of customers)
- Productivity rate measures (e.g., close rate)
- Milestones

Subjective or Judgement Measures:

- MBOs (objectives)
- Knowledge, skills, abilities

Financial/Production Measures

Strategic Measures

Input and Activity Measures

Subjective or Judgment Measures

FIGURE 5-1

- Input and activity measures
- Subjective or judgment measures.

Mix of Measures

To ensure a well-balanced plan, the core measures should be part of financial/production and strategic measures when possible. Input and activity and subjective or judgment measures should supplement the core design.

Financial/Production Measures

Typically, financial/production measures are the core measures in an incentive plan. They focus on sales dollars, margin or margin dollars, or units, and most often measure volume. Many plans give financial/production measures the most weight (i.e., the largest share of target incentive is linked to them). These measures should be tied directly to the success of the organization's financials. A sales incentive plan should have at least one financial or production measure, and it should be the primary measure.

Strategic Measures

Strategic measures also are considered core measures, but usually are seen as secondary to the financial/production measures. These measures deal specifically with an organization's strategic priorities and may focus on specific customers or products, or measures that drive a specific strategic priority (e.g., a customer retention factor, unit factor, customer service or quality). Often, strategic measures are not stated in absolute dollars, but include a percentage factor or ratio (e.g., retain 95 percent of base revenue). If a plan has a financial/production measure, it is common to also see a strategic measure that helps drive overall revenue or production. As with financial measures, strategic measures usually are given significant prominence or weight.

Input and Activity Measures

Activity measures focus on a representative's activities, events or milestones, such as key customer events, key sales process steps, number of qualified leads, conversations, number of sales calls and so on. Organizations may use these measures when they want to achieve major milestones or have a long sales cycle, or in cases in which more typical criteria may be difficult to measure. Input and activity measures also are used with new product launches or in new businesses when certain activities are critical to gain customer interest.

Input and activity measures are not core measures or secondary measures; they usually are considered third-tier and receive a lesser weight than either a financial or strategic measure. However, a company may decide to make an input and activity measure more prominent if the activity is a major determinant of success, or if financial or strategic measures are extremely difficult to set. Because input and activity measures do not always drive sales, it is important to closely monitor them to ensure they have the desired effect on behavior.

Subjective or Judgment Measures

Subjective or judgment measures typically relate to objectives that are less quantitative (numbers-related) and more qualitative (observed), making them somewhat tough to measure. They may include professional objectives or discretionary behaviors that a representative must demonstrate.

Subjective measures should be less prominent and have the least weight in the measurement hierarchy, as shown in Figure 5-1. Include subjective or judgment measures in a plan only to influence the sales team's behavior. To counterbalance the judgment factor, many companies will cap payouts and limit any excellence or accelerated payouts.

The Rules for Performance Measure Selection

To be effective, performance measures should be controllable, measurable, aligned and limited to three or fewer.

Controllable

Incentive measures must be controllable by the sales job. Sales representatives must:

- Have clear line of sight to the measures
- View them as attainable, even if they require stretch to achieve
- Understand the necessary actions as well as possess the capacity to take those actions
- Know exactly what they are being measured on and be able to influence the measure
- Understand how the measure links to their overall target or quota and their pay.

Essentially, the link between behavior and results must be clearly understood, attainable and tangible.

Measurable

The organization must be able to consistently and effectively determine results against a measure. The organization also needs to be confident that the measures are driving the proper behaviors. This requires:

- Reporting results regularly (e.g., monthly, quarterly) to help identify directions and trends
- Providing a view into both what has occurred and what lies ahead
- Ensuring communication about the plan is clear.

Many plans include measures that cannot be tracked back to a representative or sales team at the end of the measurement period (e.g., overall customer satisfaction, a quality factor for a division, overall corporate returns). Companies often track a financial measure to the manager level and then force-fit it to the representatives. Unfortunately, the inability to measure a representative's performance close to the point of sale or with enough frequency causes the plan to lose effectiveness. Representatives need to see how their results get credited and where they stand versus quota to reinforce appropriate selling behaviors. In fact, the higher a representative's variable pay mix, the more important it is to make the line of sight to the measures clear and unambiguous. It is important to ensure that reporting systems and processes capture the necessary data and make certain that any needed measurement-system enhancements can be implemented quickly and efficiently.

Aligned

Measures must align with the strategic business objectives of both the overall organization and the sales organization. Plan measures must tie directly to business strategy and drive overall corporate performance. Also, measures for the salesforce must align with the key objectives of the sales management team. Sales measures should align vertically and horizontally; motivate representatives, their managers and senior sales managers similarly; and drive company performance. Therefore, measures should be as similar as possible up the chain of command. Overall volume will be different, but the measures should be compatible and complementary. Pay and overall plan mechanics might differ across job roles, but clear alignment among the groups should be apparent.

Performance Measure Alignment

The following questions provide a quick check to ensure measures are aligned:

- Do performance measures reflect the sales strategy and each job's critical roles?
- Do relationships between these measures (e.g., weights, links, hurdles and multipliers) reflect the priorities of each measure?
- Does the plan communicate the desired job strategy to the employee in the simplest and clearest way possible, or is the message complicated by unnecessary measures?

Limited to Three or Fewer

A compensation plan should have no more than three measures to ensure that the sales representative is able to direct the appropriate focus to each performance measure. Too many requirements can cause a dilution of effort. Remember: Less is more.

Also, a measure should not have less than 20 percent of target incentive tied to it. Anything below 20 percent can become insignificant to representatives, inadvertently directing them away from the measure. Representatives will devote less effort because they get minimal payout for the measure. With more than three measures, it's more challenging to allocate the incentive target in a way that gives each measure enough significance and keeps the payout per measure motivational.

Consider this example: If an organization's annual incentive target of $25,000 is split equally among five measures at 20 percent each, the target payout for each measure is $5,000. Divided by 52 weeks, each measure offers just $96 per week. Assume you are paid incentive every two weeks for two weeks' performance. The actual biweekly payout is $192 for two weeks, assuming 100 percent of quota is achieved.

More measures dilute the power of the incentive. Eventually, the dollars earned per measure become irrelevant. Figure 5-2 presents some simple guidelines to help narrow measurement choices.

Weighting Measures (Share of Target Incentive)

After selecting performance measures, the next decision is how to weight, or assign a share of target incentive to, each measure. In quota-based plans, weights must total 100 percent, with each performance measure receiving a percentage or share of the target incentive. The higher the weighting, the more meaningful (or prominent) the performance measure.

As an example, Figure 5-3 shows a plan that has three measures: revenue, product mix, new account revenue. Of the three, revenue (at 50 percent) has the greatest weight; product mix is next with 30 percent; and new account revenue has the least weight at 20 percent. The target incentive for this representative is $10,000. Therefore, each measure has its own target that represents the weight multiplied by the total target incentive.

When assigning weights, keep in mind:

- No one measure should be weighted less than 20 percent at target.

FIGURE 5-2

Guidelines for Assessing Measurement Options

	Rule	Exceptions
Effort versus Result	Measure results whenever practical.	• New reps • Extremely long selling cycle • Certain activities scientifically linked to results
Level of Measurement	The closer to the individual, the more motivational.	• Team focus needed
Absolute versus Quota	While absolute is easier, quotas direct performance more effectively.	• Every sale "new" • No territories/territories equal • Impossible to forecast
Focus (for goal-based measures)	Internal measures are typically used due to information availability.	• Good external data sources available
Time Frame	The time frame that reps can reasonably be expected to influence the performance measure(s) selected.	• Maintaining meaningful payout levels
Hard versus Soft	"Hard" quantitative data are typically used.	• Long selling cycles • Relationship-based positions • Contributions to team selling

FIGURE 5-3

Illustrative Weights and Targets

Measure	Weight	Target Incentive
Revenue	50%	$5,000
Product Mix	30%	$3,000
New Account Revenue	20%	$2,000
TOTAL	100%	$10,000

- It is preferable to weight measures differently to communicate priorities and direction (e.g., in a two-measure plan, weights of 60 percent and 40 percent are better than 50 percent and 50 percent).

- Weights should reflect the significance of the activities/behaviors for the job; that is, the weight assigned to a measure should reflect the effort desired for that measure.

- Any overall business measures or sales objectives should be considered and prioritized when assigning weightings to ensure that the performance measures drive the desired behavior within the salesforce. This is especially true if the corporate objectives are rolled down to the representative level and representatives have individual goals and assignments. If the objective is an aggregate corporate number that a representative has little effect on, a lighter weight may be appropriate.

In commission-based plans, higher commission rates typically are established for the more heavily weighted or desirable performance measures or products. This helps accentuate achievement in those areas. As shown in Figure 5-4, Product C clearly has the most desirable measure, and likely the most challenging to sell. Therefore, it receives the highest weighting and greatest commission rate. And, as shown in Figure 5-5, components and weightings may differ by job. Figure 5-6 helps determine whether a measure meets the selection criteria. To use this chart, insert potential measures and then assess whether they are controllable, measurable and strategic.

FIGURE 5-4

Weights in Commission Plans

Product	Target Revenue	Commission Rate	Target Incentive	Weighting
A	$160K	3%	$4,800	20%
B	$168K	5%	$8,400	35%
C	$180K	6%	$10,800	45%
TOTAL	$508K		$24,000	

FIGURE 5-5

Illustrative Components and Weights by Position

Position	Pay Mix	Plan Components	Measure Weighting
Major Account Manager	70/30	Total Account Revenue	50%
		Strategic Product Revenue	30%
		New Account Bonus	20%
Sales Executive	60/40	Total Account Revenue	100%
Inside Sales/ Telesales Rep	80/20	Team Revenue	100%
Market Development Rep	75/25	Lead Generation	50%
		Forecast Bonus	30%
		New Business Bonus	20%

FIGURE 5-6

Evaluating Performance Measures

Measure	Performance Measure Criteria		
	Controllable	Measurable	Aligned with Strategy
Corporate revenue			
Regional revenue			
Product revenue			
Profit/margin dollars			
Retention revenue			
Penetration revenue			
Acquisition revenue			
Customer satisfaction			
Customer penetration			
Product penetration			
Number of sales proposals			
Number of qualified leads			

6 Mechanics, Links and Quotas

Payout formulae, payment terms, caps, thresholds and links are where the rubber meets the road in compensation plan design. These are a plan's mechanics, which form the underpinnings of plan design. Proper understanding and use of mechanics and links helps ensure sales representatives have clear line of sight from their performance and subsequent results to the payouts generated from those results. Mechanics and links also help ensure balance in a plan by motivating representatives to focus on the complete job, not just certain objectives or components. This chapter discusses:

- Different sales plan mechanics, payout formulae or mechanical elements, and how they work
- Why and when to employ different mechanics.

The Importance of Mechanics

The next component of the Optimal Sales Compensation Design Process, mechanics, links and quotas, brings the compensation plan into focus and ensures pay elements and measures are brought together in a way that spurs the salesforce to accomplish critical objectives and earn rewards commensurate with their accomplishments.

"Mechanics" is a buzzword used to describe the inner workings of an incentive plan design. A plan's mechanics create the structure and details for how a compensation plan actually pays out given a representative's level of achievement. Depending on the incentive plan structure, mechanics may include payout formulae and/or payout tables that correspond to results against quota or target.

A "link" refers to how each mechanic or design component operates in parallel with the other, or based on the different levels of performance achieved. A link between components allows an organization to ensure that sales representatives have balanced performance across their various objectives. Typically, when plans have links, a representative is required to achieve a certain level of performance across multiple components before earning higher pay (e.g., excellence pay). Earnings may be flat over 100 percent of quota or target on Measure 1 (i.e., no accelerated pay) until Measure 2 also reaches 100 percent of target. Once results are more than 100 percent for Measure 2, the acceleration kicks in.

Mechanics and links can add complexity and, too often, confusion to a plan. The moment sales representatives learn about a new plan, they take out their calculators to see how the plan will affect their bottom line. They study the plan's mechanics to determine how all components link. This helps them understand — in real terms — how the plan will affect them and which behaviors are necessary to achieve the greatest rewards. If representatives don't quickly grasp how the plan works and what they can earn, it may mean the plan is overengineered — either there's too much going on, or the mechanics are too complex. When designing a plan, leave out those extra bells and whistles. Too often, these add-ons create unnecessary complexities that garble the message. You can't control everything. Leave some of the management to the managers.

When considering certain plan mechanics, ask yourself: *Do plan mechanics and corresponding link requirements encourage peak performance, or do they overregulate or hinder achievement by adding too much burden?*

There are many types of mechanics or links in sales compensation plans. Some are common in most plans; others are used in select situations. Mechanics and links can be the payout formulae that tie a plan to the sales targets or commission rates. They also may include performance modifiers or payment terms that ultimately dictate how and when a representative gets paid. There are four general categories of mechanics and links. Figure 6-1 outlines the type of mechanics that typically are used in sales compensation plans.

Mechanics of Commissions

Commission plan mechanics pay a rate, dollar amount or percent based on a representative's sales. Commission plans have the following characteristics:

- Revenue or product focus
- Simple performance measurement

FIGURE 6-1

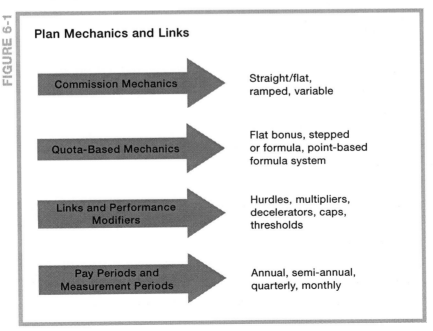

Plan Mechanics and Links

Commission Mechanics	→	Straight/flat, ramped, variable
Quota-Based Mechanics	→	Flat bonus, stepped or formula, point-based formula system
Links and Performance Modifiers	→	Hurdles, multipliers, decelerators, caps, thresholds
Pay Periods and Measurement Periods	→	Annual, semi-annual, quarterly, monthly

- High sales-representative prominence
- Short selling cycle
- Representative control over sales and sales volume
- Medium to high volume of sales.

Advantages
Generally, commission plans are clear and straightforward, with clear line of sight. Representatives find them easy to understand and can equate their immediate earnings to their performance. Commission-based plans can create a more sales-focused culture in which performance is based upon dollars earned. Many organizations find it easier to emphasize multiple products by using differentiated or varied payouts or commission rates for different products. Also, sales organizations generally believe that you can never overpay, as rates are based on and tied to the sale of an individual product or direct revenue attainment. The company knows exactly what it is paying for because each product sale or revenue dollar has a specific rate tied to its attainment.

Disadvantages
A sales organization may lose some ability to drive specific behaviors because representatives will sell where the money is, focusing their efforts on sales that yield the highest (or easiest) commissions. Also, commission plans usually pay from the first sale or first dollar sold, so there is no minimum threshold of acceptable performance that must be reached for earnings to start. A commission plan typically pays on all sales, even if representatives have sold very little and have not covered any fixed costs or salary.

Commission plans can be perceived and function as an aggressive sales plan. They may reinforce bad behaviors if representatives cherry pick and fail to penetrate accounts. Also, commission plans can create a "slamming" environment in which a representative sells a product just to get the incentive, but pays little attention to the fulfillment of the sale or collection of customer payments. To ensure fulfillment and collections happen, many companies try to keep representatives focused on the entire sales process, holding them accountable for booking the sale, shipping the product and ensuring the customer pays.

In addition, commission plans make it difficult to factor in ability, tenure and potential. All representatives are treated equally, which may be right or wrong for an organization given the business and sales strategy.

I learned about the complications of mechanics early in my career. A company I worked for had a commission-based plan that rewarded representatives for the customer commitment, not the actual amount sold. This company sold nontangible Internet advertising/media services. The incentive plan paid a commission for the amount of leads each customer might receive based on the advertisement in his/her channel. Customers did not pay for space, but paid based upon responses to their ads. A customer had to make a nonbinding commitment to purchase the leads in advance, but ultimately did not have to pay if the leads did not materialize. There was very little risk for customers to say they wanted to purchase 2,000 leads versus the standard 750 leads. In fact, a customer would pay less for a high-volume commitment. On the other hand, the representatives were paid for the customers' nonbinding commitment, not the final amount received.

After about six months on this plan, the company quickly realized that it had trained the representatives too well. The plan was hugely successful, as representatives sold very large lead packages to customers — well beyond the company's estimates. The problem was, while representatives were selling the packages and getting paid when a customer signed the contract, the leads from the ads were not materializing, or took a very long time to qualify as "real" leads. The company was making large payouts for representatives for future sales, or for "optimistically enthusiastic" sales, as the COO observed. Yet the actual revenue to the firm did not materialize. It did not take a consultant to realize any new plan and subsequent mechanics had to link customer payment or collection to the commission payouts.

Commission Payout Approaches

Typically there are three types of commission plans:

- **Straight/flat commission:** In a straight/flat plan, representatives are paid a specific percentage of the total dollar value of the revenue sold (e.g., 4 percent, as shown in Figure 6-2) or dollar amount per sale or unit (e.g., $250, as shown in Figure 6-2).

- **Ramped commission:** A ramped commission pays a variable percentage or rate, or a dollar value as volume increases. The increase may ramp up either with or without a formal target or quota. If it is purely based on volume, rates will ramp up as volume increases. This is referred to as a variable target mechanic. Other ramped commission plans may have a threshold that must be achieved to earn the percentage or dollar payout. This is called a variable target and threshold-based mechanic. In Figure 6-3, the commission rate increases according to the percent of quota achieved. In Figure 6-4, commission dollars increase as more units are sold.

- **Variable commission:** A variable commission rate or dollar amount is established based on the type of product sold, account sold to or percent of margin achieved. A plan may have different commission rates for different performance measures or indicators. In Figure 6-5, each product has a different commission rate.

Quota Plans

In a quota plan, representatives have performance targets that they are expected to achieve. To earn target incentives, representatives must achieve the quota.

FIGURE 6-2

Example of a Straight/Flat Commission

Revenue	
Percent of Revenue	Dollars per Unit
4%	$250

Characteristics of quota plans include:

- Variations in quotas by territory and potential
- Multiple performance measures
- Complex selling processes
- Low to moderate sales representative prominence
- Desire to be more directive about what should be accomplished over a designated period of time
- Ability to establish goals or standards
- Less control over sale and sales volume.

FIGURE 6-3

Example of a Ramped Commission, Based on Revenue

Revenue	
Percent of Quota	Commission Rate
120% and Above	7%
100%–119%	6%
80%–99%	4%
0%–79%	2%

FIGURE 6-4

Example of a Ramped Commission, Based on Units Sold

Units	
Units Sold	Commission Dollars (per unit)
31 and above	$300
26–30	$250
21–25	$150
10–20	$100

Advantages

Generally, quota plans are used in more mature situations in which a history of performance exists for representatives and the organization. This track record gives the sales organization a better handle on representative capability and potential performance, allowing management to allocate the complete potential of a territory, product line or sales objective to the sales representatives.

With a quota plan, the organization can cascade its financial goals to the sales organization. The tighter the alignment, the better the allocation and performance correlation between management and representatives. In addition, quotas enable sales organizations to more easily factor in a representative's skill level, tenure, location and overall ability to meet job requirements.

Disadvantages

Quotas may obscure line of sight because of the lapse between when the sale is made and when dollars are credited. Consequently, representatives may lose sight of the alignment between the sale and its payout. Also, accurately setting quotas can be challenging if there is insufficient or unsubstantial data for determining allocations for new products, territories or overall growth goals. If these difficulties lead to inaccurate targets, an organization may pay out too much or too little — and either scenario can create a huge issue for both the company and representatives.

FIGURE 6-5

Example of a Variable Commission

Percent of Quota	Revenue		
	Product A	Product B	Product C
100% and above	2.0%	4.0%	6.0%
0%–99%	1.5%	2.5%	3.5%

Quota Payout Approaches

There are multiple approaches to determining the best payout method for a quota-based plan. Some of the most widely used include:

- **Step or formula bonus:** The percentage of target incentive earned corresponds to the level of quota achieved. The payout percentage "steps up" at determined intervals as performance accelerates. Payouts vary based upon percent of quota attained. In Figure 6-6, the percent of target incentive increases for each level of attainment.

- **Individual commission rate:** A variable payout percentage of target incentive is paid based on the percentage of quota achieved. The individual commission rate is based on the ratio between the target incentive and quota. As shown in Figure 6-7, commission rates will vary by representative based upon each representative's actual quota.

FIGURE 6-6

Example of a Step or Formula Bonus

Revenue	
Percent of Quota	Percent of Target Incentive
120% and above	200%
110%	150%
100%	100%
90%	75%
80%	50%
0% – 79%	0

- **Point-based formula system:** In this system, results achieved correspond to a formula or amount of points that, in turn, determine the incentive payout. Each performance measure may have a different formula. Figure 6-8 shows three different products with different point-based formulas. The higher the attainment on each product, the higher the point value; the more points achieved, the more incentive earned.

- **Bonus matrix:** In a bonus matrix, the combined results of two performance measures determine the incentive payout. It is used to tightly link competing objectives (e.g., revenue and profit). Matrices may be complex to design and decipher, especially if measures have unequal weightings or one measure has more prominence than the other.

Figure 6-9 illustrates a bonus matrix. In the example, if both profit and revenue quotas are met (100 percent each), the target payout is 100 percent of the target incentive. If results on the profit measure are 90 percent of quota and revenue results are 100 percent, the payout is 80 percent of target incentive.

FIGURE 6-7

Example of an Individual Commission Rate

Individual

$$\text{Individual Commission Rate} = \frac{\text{Individual Target Commission}}{\text{Individual Quota}}$$

Examples:

Rep #1

$$\text{Individual Commission Rate} = \frac{\$40,000}{\$1,200,000} = 3.3\%$$

Rep #2

$$\text{Individual Commission Rate} = \frac{\$40,000}{\$950,000} = 4.2\%$$

Example of a Points-Based Formula System

Step 1

Revenue					
Product A		Product B		Product C	
Percent of Quota	Points	Percent of Quota	Points	Percent of Quota	Points
130%	25	110%	25	120%	50
120%	20	107%	20	114%	40
110%	15	105%	15	107%	30
100%	12.5	100%	12.5	100%	25
90%	10	90%	10	90%	20
80%	5	80%	5	80%	10
70%	—	70%	—	70%	—

Step 2

Total Points	Percent of Target Incentive	
90-100	250%	
80-89	200%	← Excellence Point
70-79	150%	
60-69	120%	
50-59	100%	← Target
40-49	90%	
30-39	80%	
20-29	70%	← Threshold
0-19	0	

FIGURE 6-8

- **Flat bonus:** A flat bonus is straightforward: A flat dollar amount is earned for achieving quota or the specified performance objective. In Figure 6-10, the payout is $25,000 for selling five accounts with revenue above $100,000.

Quota Setting and Allocation

There are multiple methods for effectively setting quotas. Figure 6-11 shows the four most popular methods.

Questions to Ask if Using Quotas

- Are objectives set and allocated to the salesforce in an equitable manner?

- Do quotas create "performance penalties" for top performers, or create a "welfare state" for mediocrity?

- Does the sales organization buy in to quotas through a process that uses its input in a clear and consistent way?

- Do quotas account for variations in territory size, potential and growth?

- If quotas require future adjustments, are clear guidelines in place for conditions and approvals?

FIGURE 6-9

Example of a Bonus Matrix

		Matrix			
		Percent Target Incentive			
110%	150%	163%	175%	188%	200%
105%	115%	127%	138%	150%	188%
100%	80%	90%	100%	138%	175%
95%	45%	55%	90%	127%	163%
90%	10%	45%	80%	115%	150%
	80%	90%	100%	110%	120%

Profit Percent to Quota

Revenue Percent to Quota

FIGURE 6-10

Example of a Flat Bonus

Flat Accounts	
Objective	Incentive
5 New Accounts Sold (>$100,000 Annual Revenue)	$25,000

FIGURE 6-11

Methods for Setting Quotas

Least Complex

Historic Allocation
- Pro-rata allocation based on last year's performance
- Simple process
- Doesn't account for territory potential
- Creates a "performance penalty"; best carry the burden

Adjusted Value
- Pro-rata allocation modified by factors (e.g., market opportunity, penetration, competition, representatives' experience)
- Creates equitable objectives
- Easy to administer

Algorithm
- Hurdles, multipliers, matrices-calculated goal based on predictive variables (e.g., accounts, potential, current revenue, etc.)
- Effective for large numbers of small accounts
- "Black box" effect may be validated with other methods

Account Planning
- Individual account evaluation
- Driven by the representative and sales manager
- Effective for small number of large accounts

Most Complex

Links and Performance Modifiers

Plan links ensure that payouts and strategy are properly aligned. They may take a variety of forms (e.g., performance gates, hurdles, qualifiers, matrices, tie-in qualifiers). Regardless of what they are called, they do the same thing: require minimum performance on one measure to earn a payout on another measure (assuming results are at or over target on the second measure).

In Figure 6-12, profit and revenue measures are linked. Representatives cannot earn any overtarget or excellence payouts on the revenue measure until they exceed target on the profit measure. In this way, the revenue measure's excellence is linked to the profit targets. Representatives would earn up to target payout on the revenue measure but not more (even if sales exceed 100 percent) until they reach 100 percent or greater on the profit measure. (Note: In some instances, companies will pay a flat payout above target based upon performance on the first measure [rate at 100 percent of target] but not pay the accelerated amount [more than 100 percent of target] until the second measure is achieved.)

Performance modifiers also help align performance with strategy. They modify payouts to protect or ensure strategy is aligned with pay philosophies or performance. They also bring balance and equity to payouts to maintain the integrity of the plan's design. Common types of performance modifiers include:

Bonus multiplier: An increased payout that is applied to target incentive for exceptional results on an assigned goal. Performance on a second measure can trigger additional payout on the first measure. Lower performance on the second measure may cause a negative adjustment to the measure on earnings. (See Figure 6-13.)

Incentive payout caps: A limit or ceiling on payouts. Caps safeguard against overpayment and help ensure the company does not exceed its compensation budget if performance surpasses quotas. The use of caps stirs strong debate in many companies.

Figure 6-14 shows how incentive caps work. In the "no cap" graph, pay is unlimited, allowing the representative to continue earning incentives as long as he/she continues selling. In the second graph, pay is capped at 150 percent, so even if sales continue, the representative will not earn more once the cap kicks in.

Links

FIGURE 6-12

| Percent of Profit Quota | Profit and Revenue | | | |
	Percent of Revenue Quota	Percent of Target Incentive (Under Profit Target)	Percent of Target Incentive (Over Profit Target)	
			200%	← Excellence
		100%	166%	
		100%	133%	
100%	100%	100%	100%	← Target
90%	90%	90%	90%	
80%	80%	80%	80%	← Threshold
0-79%	0-79%	0	0	

To Cap or Not to Cap?

Caps bring out the emotions, with reasonable argument to be made on both sides.

Making a Case for:

Uncapped Earnings Opportunities

- Motivates peak performance and creates perception (and reality) of unlimited opportunity

- Creates success stories that the company can share to create excitement, as reps can earn as much as possible

- Requires financial plan modeling to keep costs within acceptable parameters

- Requires a management culture that welcomes high earners. This means being OK with reps earning more than managers.

Capping Earnings Opportunities

- Creates a controlled pay atmosphere, as there is limited payout opportunity

- Useful if financial modeling is unreliable — a company knows it will only pay out to a certain level

- May be important if goals are set with little reliable information

- Used in environments of production constraints — reps can't sell more than capacity allows.

Thresholds and Deceleration

A threshold is a minimum performance level that must be achieved so incentive earnings can start accruing. Typically, either no incentives are earned up to threshold, or earnings are severely decelerated until the threshold is met (e.g., plan pays 10 percent below a threshold but 20 percent above the threshold). Commission plans typically have no threshold, as they pay from dollar one.

Advantages

Thresholds are particularly useful when representatives have a stream of business, and a certain percentage of that business is predictable or recurring. The larger the percentage of predictable/recurring revenue, the higher the threshold can be. Thresholds

Shifting Payouts to High Producers

To help fund accelerated payments or stay within fixed compensation budgets, companies may shift payouts from low producers to high producers, effectively acting like Robin Hood in reverse. The figure below shows a common performance distribution curve. The organization has 10 percent of its representatives at or below a threshold and 5 percent to 10 percent at or above the excellence level. Sixty percent to 75 percent are at or above target. The organization could make no or minimal payouts to the bottom performers in order to make funds available for those who reach or exceed the excellence level.

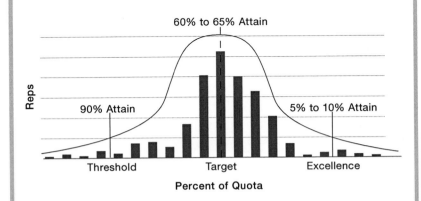

Payments are taken from the reps below threshold and given to the reps above target or over excellence.

usually are set at or below the 10th percentile of performers. In this way, they can create an artificial target for lower performers to strive toward.

Disadvantages

Without a threshold, representatives can earn from dollar one — a feature that can be highly motivational. Even low performance is better than no performance. Remember that "no threshold" plans require financial modeling to ensure that the dollars paid out will be within acceptable ratios of dollars brought in. Companies that don't use a threshold may have lower commission levels at lower levels of performance.

Figure 6-15 illustrates and explains three common types of thresholds.

FIGURE 6-13

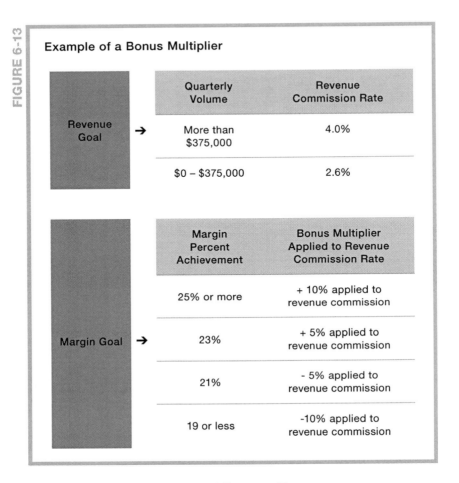

Example of a Bonus Multiplier

Revenue Goal →	Quarterly Volume	Revenue Commission Rate
	More than $375,000	4.0%
	$0 – $375,000	2.6%

Margin Goal →	Margin Percent Achievement	Bonus Multiplier Applied to Revenue Commission Rate
	25% or more	+ 10% applied to revenue commission
	23%	+ 5% applied to revenue commission
	21%	- 5% applied to revenue commission
	19 or less	-10% applied to revenue commission

Measurement Periods and Payout Frequency

A plan's measurement period specifies the time period over which performance is measured. Standard periods include monthly, quarterly or semiannually. These interim periods usually roll up into a longer, cumulative period, typically a year (cumulative year-to-date results). With a cumulative period, companies typically hold excellence payouts back until total cumulative results are tabulated. Representatives do receive pay for performance up to target for each segment. Paying for cumulative results aligns pay with the attainment of annual goals — an approach favored by the finance department. Yet, it has a motivational downside: Representatives may give up if they fall behind quota early in the year.

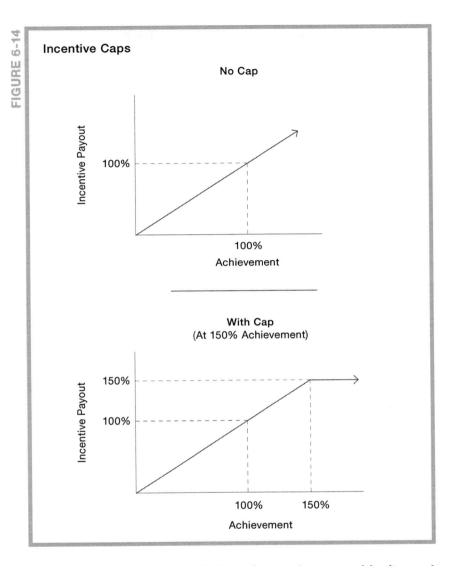

FIGURE 6-14

Incentive Caps

Some plans employ a stand-alone feature (e.g., monthly discrete) in which each measurement period stands on its own and is not tied to another period. This can keep top sellers in the game, but also can lead to overpayment if most monthly goals are achieved but the overall total doesn't add up to the annual goal. A similar approach is to measure results quarterly and include a year-end measure for annual goal achievement. In a "fifth quarter" approach, earnings are held back and paid when results for all quarters are in. If attainment is high in all four quarters, the incentives held in reserve are paid out.

Payout frequency denotes how often incentives are paid (e.g., biweekly, monthly, quarterly). Factors to consider include the payment size, administrative burden and feasibility. Can the plan be implemented and paid consistently without a large burden?

Mechanics Guidelines

This step of incentive design brings so many features into play, it can seem overwhelming. The following guidelines can keep the design process on track:

- Keep plan mechanics simple, effective and easy to understand, while providing for enticing upside potential.

- Finalize plan mechanics only after finalizing decisions on the measures, upside and excellence points

- In working through the decisions, be sure to weight the following factors:
  - Degree of seller prominence
  - Extent to which the volume is seller-driven versus recurring revenue
  - Equities/inequities of territory and account distribution
  - Need or desire for plan flexibility
  - Integrity of data and planning process
  - Willingness to do the work required by the quota-setting process.

FIGURE 6-15

Potential Approaches to Setting Thresholds

Soft Threshold Formula

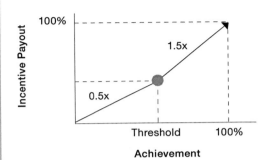

Description: The company pays higher rates as achievement increases (aka progressive formula).

Hard Threshold Formula

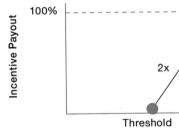

Description: The company pays incentives on achievement above assigned minimum performance level once achieved.

Step Threshold Formula

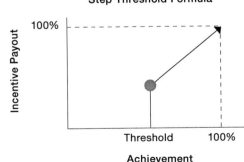

Description: The company pays on all sales after a required minimum performance level has been achieved (aka step-up formula).

A Quota Quiz

Match the following summaries with the performance distribution graphs in Figure 6-16.

Which chart shows:

1. Poor quota-setting, effective allocation?
2. Effective quota-setting, effective allocation?
3. Boom, bust or performance penalty?
4. Effective quota-setting, poor allocation?

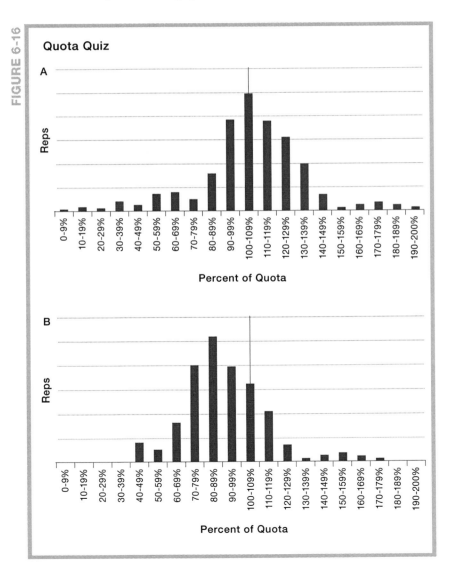

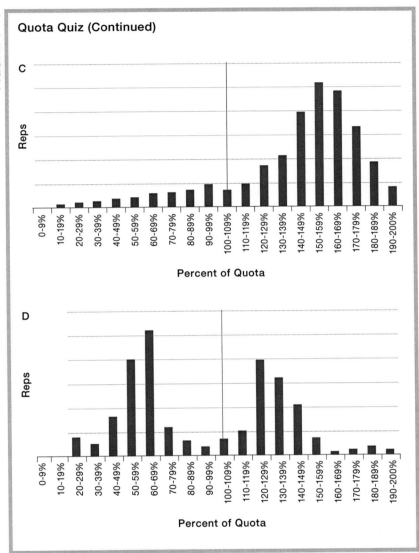

Answers:
1. B
2. A
3. D
4. C

Note: Chapter 8 explains how a distribution analysis can help judge a plan's effectiveness.

7 Implementation and Communication

The best design inadequately communicated may not deliver as expected. Effective communication and implementation helps the organization understand the plan and behaviors needed to achieve results. This chapter provides an overview of optimum communication and rollout focusing on:

- Why communication is so important
- What a successful communications road map entails
- How to use communication materials to create excitement and heighten motivation.

Implementation and communication form the critical sixth step in the sales incentive design process. No matter how elegant, well-thought and seemingly intuitive a sales compensation design appears, if it is not properly communicated and rolled out, it runs the risk of being misunderstood, ignored and/or underachieved. Even the best compensation plans must be "sold" to sales representatives and sales management. If representatives do not have a clear idea of what they do and why they do it, they may continue past patterns rather than change their behavior to take on the new set of challenges required to meet the new sales objectives. Even worse, if they do not understand how and why they are getting paid, they may totally discredit the new plan right from the start.

Several years ago, I completed an intensive global sales compensation project with a major software company. Our team had worked meticulously conducting interviews and data analysis, and vetting design features to develop a strongly aligned compensation plan. The client's leadership team and sales management were unanimous in their support of the new plan.

When we moved from design to implementation, the company decided to handle communication and rollout on its own. At one of our final meetings, we discussed in some detail the steps of implementation planning, rollout and communication, including timing, materials and overall messaging. When the new quarter was under way, I called the project manager to see how the new plan was working. She was clearly stressed. She commented that she was putting out fires and didn't have time to talk. Another contact was more than forthcoming: "Our plans are good, but no one understands them."

The salesforce had received a plan summary that was short on background, leaving out the "why" and the "what's in it for me." Adding to the miscommunication, the plan was rolled out after the new period started, so the representatives started the new year uncertain about how they would get paid. "I tell you, Joe," the client said, "we made a mess of our great work, and I'm not sure we can recover."

Rules for Effective Communication

To ensure that the new compensation plans hit the ground running, communication must be timely and effective:

- Even the best compensation plans must be sold to the field.
- Without a good communications plan, even positive plan changes can fail.
- Do not underestimate the value of a comprehensive communications strategy.
- Incentive plan communication entails more than delivering a plan document and job description.

Pitfalls of Poor Communication

As with the software company example, the pitfalls of poor communication can result in a true setback. In the meantime, morale and sales can take a nose dive. Sales leaders commonly cite these results of ineffective communication:

- **Overall reduction of personal productivity.** Employees spend more time talking around the watercooler and less on the street selling. They are upset and concerned that the plan has changed, and they believe they are underpaid, when in reality they aren't.

- **Overall breakdown in communication.** Poor initial communication can cascade into a total avoidance of discussions about the plan on the part of sales management. If sales managers don't quite get how the plan works, they may stonewall questions or throw up their hands in confusion and join the chorus of negativity about a plan's perceived unfairness and ineffectiveness.

- **Reduction in overall corporate performance.** If the salesforce lacks a good understanding of how to perform against goals or earn more money, sales reps make take shortcuts or focus on sales that are not aligned with the business strategy. Such actions may jeopardize results over the long haul.

- **Exacerbated turnover.** Absent clarity about performance and pay, representatives may seek better opportunities elsewhere. And if performance and productivity take a hit, the turnover may be company-mandated as well as voluntary.

Communication Strategy

Any communication and implementation approach must be pragmatic and polished. It must be easy to understand, timely and communicated at all levels. At a high level, the strategy must reinforce the business reasons for the change and emphasize management's commitment to these changes. The strategy should help the sales organization understand and personalize the rationale and benefits of the new pay process. Also, communication should include models and examples that support and encourage behaviors required to support the pay plan changes. The following characteristics of effective communication should be the cornerstone of sales communication strategy:

- **Personalized and low-cost.** Targeted, personalized information can be distributed across large populations without losing the richness of the message or increasing costs.

- **Just enough.** Strike the right balance between too much and not enough. Communications should outline the why, what and how in sufficient detail.

- **Always current.** It is critical to get information to people when they need it. Communication about a new plan should precede the start of the measurement period. Performance results should be available within a reasonable period.

- **Always accessible.** Supply plan details and performance results in a mode that is easily accessed.

Six Steps for Implementing and Communicating Sales Incentives

Step	Considerations
1. Define the objectives. What message, goals and behaviors do you want to reinforce?	• How does the new plan support the organization's strategic goals? • What behaviors are you trying to reinforce? • What resistance do you expect? • What are the concerns/goals of the audience you are addressing? • What actions do you want people to take as a result of the message? • What is the change's ultimate outcome?
2. Evaluate employee understanding. What is the current situation?	• What has already been communicated about the plan changes? • How well do employees understand the current plans and/or anticipated changes? • How well do employees understand the behaviors necessary for success under the current plan and/or the new plan? • How do employees feel about the pay process itself? • What kind of accountability do managers have in communicating the plan changes?

3. Develop communication strategy. What is the best overall approach?	• Who is/are the audience(s)?
	  - Job roles
	  - Job level
	  - Organization.
	• What information should be communicated to each audience?
	  - Key messages
	  - Appropriate level of detail.
	• When should communications start and end?
	• How often should messages be communicated?

4. Determine the media or tools. What communication vehicles are most appropriate?	• E-mail • Voice mail • Text message • Intranet • Brochure • Handbook • Meetings • Large- and/or small-group presentations • DVD.
5. Implement the plan. What are the components and timing of rollout?	Develop a plan to orchestrate rollout (see Figure 7-1), specifying the components or phases of the implementation and the timing of each.
6. Measure program success. Was the program successful?	An effective evaluation program determines: • Plan rollout effectiveness • Employee understanding • Employee satisfaction • Alignment with business strategy • Correlation between performance and rewards.

Sample Implementation Plan

Work Steps	Jun	Jul	Aug	Sept	Oct	Nov	Dec	Jan
1. Develop Communications and Change Management Plan								
Outline key stakeholders who require education and the various types of messaging needed for each.								
Identify potential communications mediums for stakeholders and the role each would play within an integrated implementation effort.								
2. Develop and Deliver Communication Materials								
Develop population-specific communications, tailoring messages and the level of detail contained within each document.								
Capture messaging through various content mediums including Webcasts, program brochures, FAQs, individual compensation statements, interactive modeling tools, etc.								
Present materials to sales and marketing leadership to ensure maximum effectiveness.								

FIGURE 7-1

Sample Implementation Plan (Continued)

Work Steps	Jun	Jul	Aug	Sept	Oct	Nov	Dec	Jan
3. Implement Plan								
Roll out final communications materials outlining new plans to appropriate audiences.	▓	▓	▓	▓	▓	▓	▓	▓
Conduct presentations aimed at particular audiences, detailing how new compensation plans work and their effects on sales.								
Provide additional support as needed, which may include contract review, revenue conversation, role transition pay arrangements, key employee retention plans, deal review board and process, crediting rules and language.								
4. Conduct Plan Design Audit, Measurement and Course Correction								
Three to six months into the performance period, conduct a thorough audit of plan effectiveness.								
If necessary, recommend changes to plan designs based on auditing results and stakeholder feedback.								

FIGURE 7-1

Successful Communication Methods

The format in which messages are communicated is just as important as the message itself. Research shows that employees prefer hearing messages directly from their supervisors, yet 80 percent of the time communication about pay comes through the grapevine. Unfortunately, what is passed on are other people's impressions — and dissatisfactions — with the program. Within the field salesforce, cascading communication can ensure understanding, dispel dissatisfaction and create a receptive, motivating environment.

Information Cascade

An effective cascade starts at the top, with the head of sales outlining the "why" — the strategy and objectives behind the plan. The key is to really engage representatives in these messages. Ideally, the new plan is rolled out at the annual sales meeting or in a salesforce Webcast, underscoring the link between the business strategy, overall sales strategy, compensation plan and required behaviors to make it all work. There is no underestimating the rah-rah effect of unveiling the annual compensation plan in conjunction with the annual sales goals, new product introductions and other key messages.

After the big-picture presentation, it is helpful to hold group forums for regional or district sales teams. These presentations should include the essential "how the plan works" information and how the plan affects the team messages that link with the strategy. These sessions can be both informational/Q&A forums as well as working sessions in which teams engage in discussing and tackling challenges.

In the field, a representative's manager should schedule a one-on-one with each representative to focus on how the individual will succeed under the new plan. The two can discuss strategies to maximize incentive opportunities.

Plan Details

Written communication should serve as a follow-up to the group and team rollout sessions. The material must echo the group messages and present the plan mechanics in clear, straightforward terms.

Brochures with plan highlights and brief, to-the-point plan documents deliver critical messages most effectively and safeguard against confusion or misunderstanding. The challenge is to be succinct yet comprehensive, hitting upon all key points critical to the success of the compensation plan and sales organization.

Many organizations use their written plan for dual purposes: communicating plan details and identifying the administrative guidelines key to the plan's governance. Such details often employ actual legal regulations, corporate policies or simple business processes that require formal language. Documents written with too many formal administrative guidelines tend to be intimidating. They can be difficult to read and/or understand. Faced with such a document, the audience often skims it, possibly missing key messages. If you are required to create this type of document, the solution may be to create two separate documents: a plan description that markets the plan and shows simple pay rates and earnings, and a companion piece that includes administrative guidelines. The guidelines may be formatted as a list of "frequently asked questions" that put the legal requirements and other dry but necessary terms and conditions into a clearer, more easily understood context.

Written communication can take various forms; the following are critical to any effective rollout:

A new plan announcement: This typically precedes a rollout and comes from senior management. This executive memorandum provides a high-level overview of the changes and often invites the field to attend a more formal presentation of the new plans. The letter typically is drafted by the design team and then revised and communicated by a senior executive. Figure 7-2 provides a sample plan announcement.

The plan document: This encompasses the key components of the new pay programs. The document typically includes plan formulae, calculation examples and relevant policy changes. The document also may include information on other benefits programs, such as the President's Club. Many companies find it valuable to include signature sheets along with the plans that include quota and pay

FIGURE 7-2

Sample Plan Announcement

To: Field Salesforce
From: SVP, Sales
Date: Nov. 28, 2009
Subject: 2010 Sales Compensation Plan

Fiscal year 2010 is a critical year for our company. Many factors, such as changes in our focus on products, selling effectiveness, customer service and market conditions, have altered the environment in which we operate. In response to these changes, we have developed a new sales incentive plan to better reward our salesforce to focus on the behaviors and results that will help us meet our fiscal year 2010 goals.

Our sales goals clearly reflect the areas of focus necessary to evolve our business and earn the leadership role of category leader in broad-line distribution and specific industry segments. We must accelerate our product categories while effectively supporting our national account business. To ensure these sales goals are met, we have done everything organizationally possible to help our sales organization contribute to our achievement in 2010 and beyond.

This new plan will allow us to more adequately reward and differentiate our high performers while better equipping us to focus on profitable sales growth and customer satisfaction. The bottom line is, we are putting in place the most effective framework possible so you are better able to focus your energy on our products and our customers. That's why I consider your ongoing support and commitment the key to our success as we enter fiscal year 2010.

I encourage you to read this plan document carefully to ensure you fully understand the key aspects of the plan as they relate to your position. Your understanding, ongoing support and commitment to the forthcoming changes are the key to our success as we enter this next phase of growth. Thank you in advance for this support.

Let's make this a maximum bonus payout year for everyone.

Onward and Upward,

John Doe
Senior Vice President, Sales

information specific for each incumbent. Signature sheets typically are used to protect the company in legal matters.

Best-in-class plan documents address four key topics: strategic objectives, plan components, compensation mechanics and incentive calculators/examples. Each topic links with the others to deliver and support a comprehensive message about the "why," "what," "how" and, most importantly, "how much" of the sales compensation plan.

Strategic Objectives: The 'Why'

Presenting a strategic overview to the compensation plan is fundamental. To buy into the plan and internalize it, sales representatives must understand the strategies and business issues facing the company, and the role and response required by the sales organization to address these strategies and contribute to the company's success.

The communication must explain both strategic and financial objectives, providing sales representatives with a clear understanding of how success is defined. The discussion of strategic objectives also should validate how the new sales compensation plan supports the organization's strategies and objectives by driving the "correct" behaviors among the salesforce. It is valuable to explain the compensation philosophy employed to develop and design the sales incentive plan. The discussion can further emphasize the key objectives and expectations for the sales organization's performance during the coming fiscal year.

If the new plan differs significantly from previous plans, explain the key changes and/or enhancements to the new plan. Depending on the audience and the shift in sales strategy or compensation design, highlight key steps and/or the players in the design process. For example, if credibility is an issue, stress that focus groups or interviews with representatives are integral to the design process. Differentiating the new plan from any past plans and explaining the methodology helps the field salespeople fully appreciate the degree to which they may need to change their sales behaviors and activities to drive the company's sales results and, ultimately, their own financial success.

Plan Components: The 'What'

Next, outline the details of the new sales incentive plan, indicating included jobs, compensation levels (base salary and incentive), pay mix, performance measures and measurement/pay periods.

Clearly defining the performance measures ensures that sales representatives understand the products, types of revenue and/or types of sales objectives on which to focus. Explain the weightings for each measure (as a percent of total sales incentive) to let representatives know where to focus their sales attention and energy. Figure 7-3 shows a simple but effective visual of what the plan components are and how they work together.

FIGURE 7-3

Displaying the Nuts and Bolts of the Sales Compensation Plan

Job Role

Brief summary description of the key responsibilities and accountabilities for the position.

- Negotiate contractual agreements with high-profile strategic clients.

- Build and strengthen relations with key clients through effective account management.

Mix and Upside

The current and recommended pay mix and upside for the position as well as the proposed payout at excellence (200 percent of target).

	Recommendation
Pay Mix	60/40
Current TTC	$100,000
Upside	3.0X
Payout at Excellence	200%

Measures and Weights

Proposed performance measures and weights.

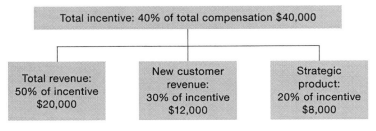

Total incentive: 40% of total compensation $40,000

Total revenue: 50% of incentive $20,000

New customer revenue: 30% of incentive $12,000

Strategic product: 20% of incentive $8,000

Plan Mechanics: The 'How'

Plan mechanics detail how incentives actually pay out given the sales representative's level of achievement. Include payout formulas and/or payout rate tables to emphasize payout levels for corresponding levels of sales achievement. Stress the selling points of the plan (e.g., no cap means unlimited earnings potential, accelerators, premiums for certain products). Figure 7-4 illustrates a payout curve that communicates the earnings opportunities available under a plan.

Payout Examples and Calculators: The 'How Much'

No communication is complete without sample calculations of incentive payouts under different sales achievement scenarios. As soon

---

Mechanics and Links

Detail of recommended mechanic type, thresholds, caps and accelerators, and measurement and payout periods.

	Recommendation		
	Measure 1	Measure 2	Measure 3
Mechanic Type	Quota	Quota	Objective
Threshold	50%	Step (50%)	No
Cap	No	No	Yes
Accelerated	Based on 100% attainment of first two measures	Based on 100% attainment of first two measures; based on MPS	
Linkage	No	No	No
Measurement	YTD annual	YTD annual	Annual
Payment	Quarterly	Quarterly	Annual

as most sales representatives learn of a new plan, they take out their calculators to understand how it will affect their bottom line, but not all of them get the calculation correct the first time. Sample calculations are a simple way to control the errors so plan participants can understand the full value and potential of the new compensation plan. Examples allow representatives to see, in real terms, how the plan will affect them and which behaviors are necessary to maximize earnings and achieve the greatest rewards. Figure 7-5 displays an illustrative compensation calculator.

If the organization plans to provide any sales performance incentives for field forces (SPIFFs) outside the new plan, communicate them separately. A separate but tandem communication can create excitement about the bells and whistles without distracting from the key messages and behaviors of the new sales compensation plan.

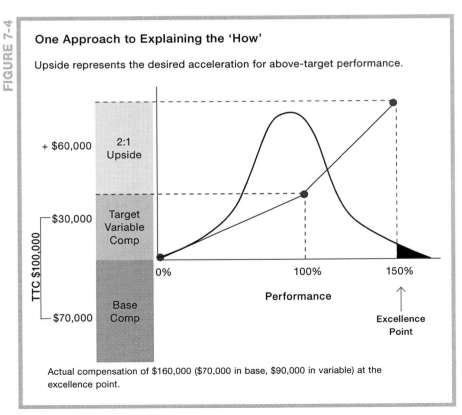

FIGURE 7-4

One Approach to Explaining the 'How'

Upside represents the desired acceleration for above-target performance.

+ $60,000 — 2:1 Upside

$30,000 — Target Variable Comp

$70,000 — Base Comp

TTC $100,000

0%   100%   150%

Performance

↑ Excellence Point

Actual compensation of $160,000 ($70,000 in base, $90,000 in variable) at the excellence point.

The communication themes and approach should align the new sales compensation plan with the organization's strategy and business issues. Communication helps sales representatives fully understand which results the sales organization must achieve in the plan year, which behaviors are required to achieve the results, and how success will be rewarded. It always is a good idea to have the plan details and guidelines available in hard copy and on the intranet for reference.

FIGURE 7-5

Compensation Plan Calculator

Major Account Manager

Total Year-to-Date Compensation	$110,000
Base Salary	$85,000
Total Target Incentive	$135,000
Total Target Compensation	$220,000
Annual Revenue Quota	$1,900,000

License Revenue

	Sales Credit	YTD Achievement	Earned Incentive
Q1	$400,000	21%	$17,053
Q2	$550,000	50%	$23,447
Q3			
Q4			
Total	$950,000	50%	$40,500

Semi-Annual Bonus

	Semi-Annual Revenue Target	Sales Credit	YTD Achievement	Earned Incentive
Q1 and Q2	$950,000	$950,000	50%	$27,000
Q3 and Q4	$950,000			
Total	$1,900,000	$950,000	50%	$27,000

FIGURE 7-5

Compensation Plan Calculator (Continued)

New Account Bonus

	Achievement	Earned Incentive
Q1	0	$0
Q2	0	$0
Q3	0	$0
Q4	0	$0
Total	0	$0

Total Incentive Compensation

	Earned Incentive	YTD Achievement
Q1	$17,053	13%
Q2	$50,447	50%
Q3		
Q4		
Total	$67,500	50%

Quota Achievement versus Total Variable Payout

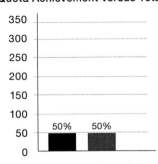

8 Plan Evaluation and Next-Cycle Planning

Plan design doesn't end after rollout; it morphs into evaluation. This chapter discusses the key performance indicators, measures and analytics that ensure a plan is working properly, and it explains how to put the proper evaluation sequence in motion to test a plan or assess its effectiveness. Topics include:

- What to look for when evaluating the sales compensation plan
- How to start the evaluation (i.e., analyses to perform and the types of data needed to model the plan's functionality and costs).

A sales manager once told me, "If compensation consultants were really smart, they'd figure out that the quickest and best way to determine whether a plan design works is to look at the shoes. If sales representatives' shoes are new and shiny with no scuffs, it means they are taking care of their feet. If they are taking care of their feet, they have money. If they have money, it means they are being paid. If they are being paid, it means the compensation plan is working. If the plan is working, it means you did a good job with your design ... nothing more to be said. You don't need any magic numbers or fancy spreadsheets; you just need to see fancy shoes."

If only it were that easy.

While shoes may tell a story, figuring out how well a plan is working requires analyzing pay and performance data to learn whether the plan's mechanics are pushing the right behaviors to create the sales results the organization needs.

Evaluation is the critical final step in the sales incentive design process. A thorough, consistent review can help reveal, avoid or prevent issues before a plan is rolled out, or while it is in play. Overpayments, underpayments, high cost of sales, poor performance distributions, plan "gaming" and so on are all typical compensation problems. While these problems can never be totally avoided or prevented, a tight evaluation process with the right analytics helps confirm what is happening with the plan and whether course corrections are needed before moving forward.

Tailor Analytics to the User Group

When analyzing a plan, think about what information will help the various stakeholders who will have different wants and needs. Consider:

- Field sales representatives want to know about their own produc-tivity and earnings. They need information about their sales results, performance against quota and individual earnings.

- Sales directors look at territories to see if things are moving in the right direction and, if not, which levers to pull to redirect behavior. They need information about sales representative performance versus peers, product placement and market potential — informa-tion that enables them to adjust their performance messages to the field to get representatives on track with territory goals.

- Regional directors look at strategic indicators that drive the sales organization. They need information related to performance versus goals, product market share, strategic initiatives and overall orga-nizational performance against goals.

Sales compensation analysis requires three views:

- **Overall financial picture:** How is the plan functioning and what are the costs (i.e., salesforce earnings and the company's return on that investment)?

- **Performance against overall objectives:** Is the plan driving the right behaviors and functioning as designed?

- **Differentiation of payouts based on performance:** Are the top earners the top performers?

Data Collection

Evaluation begins with data collection. Data needs are similar whether you are trying to judge how a plan has performed in the past year or are modeling a new plan design. Base pay, incentive pay and all related performance data that drive the incentive payments at the sales-representative and sales-manager levels all are needed.

- Collect data for both the current plan year and, at a minimum, one year prior. Try to isolate the same period in each year to control for any cyclical events (e.g., customer buying cycles) that might cause the plan to pay out more or less dollars in a certain time frame. When comparing performance years, try as much as possible to compare incumbents who were full participants in both years.

- Collect performance and compensation data by plan measure, including separate results for different payout mechanics, if applicable. When modeling a new plan design, use the prior year's performance data to see what earnings that level of performance would produce under the new plan design (e.g., if a representative performed at 85 percent of goal, use those results for the new design components). Historical performance allows a look at how much a plan would have cost and/or how much a representative would have made if the new plan design had been in place in the prior period(s).

Figure 8-1 shows a sample data request, identifying the quantitative data needed to run key analytics (discussed later in this chapter) and the qualitative data related to the overall strategy. Remember that this is the ideal wish list; not all the information may be attainable, but the list gives an idea of the type of information that is helpful to know before launching the design of a new plan, modeling a proposed plan design or assessing the effectiveness of a plan that's been operational for a year or more.

Compensation Analytical Metric Dashboard

The most successful organizations use six analytics to judge a plan's effectiveness. Together, these analytics form a compensation dashboard that allows a view into what is driving representatives' performance — where they are headed and where they have been. Using both views and the six analytics helps build a robust evaluation and obtain great assessment information.

It is important to note that the analytics can be performed in any situation before a new plan is implemented to test the plan design and ensure the mechanics will create the necessary dynamics and results, or to assess how a plan has been performing year over year, or in one isolated year. (See "The Six Analytics.")

PAR Analysis

A PAR analysis is a must-do, both to test a new plan design or a plan that has been in place for a year or more. This review examines how an organization grows its revenue:

- Penetration revenue (P): increased revenue from existing customers
- Acquisition revenue (A): new revenue from new customers
- Retention revenue (R): revenue that is renewed on an annual basis.

A PAR analysis indicates how a region, business unit and individual representative achieve objectives and grow accounts or business. It also shows the amount of churn (i.e., lost revenue or accounts) that occurs in a specific period. The analysis helps the organization ensure

FIGURE 8-1

Sample Data Request

Data Type	Specific Item	
Qualitative Data	• Copy of current sales compensation plans, including all plan descriptions and performance criteria (current year and previous years, if different) • Job profiles/descriptions • Company business plan document • Field training documents	• Field presentations • Marketing plans • Recognition program documents • Other contest/product rewards and other incentive program documentation • Organization charts • Exit interview information
Quantitative Data	• YTD pay and performance data by incumbent for current and at least one past year • YTD revenue and/or profit by customer/account (as available) for current and at least one past year • Organization- and/or region-level performance data • Sales forecast vs. actual by company, business unit, and product for current and at least one past year	• Relevant performance reports that are provided to the sales organization on a regular basis • Headcount by role and location • Turnover data • Currency conversion rates used for revenue crediting and compensation

General/Demographic Information	Pay and Performance Information (on an Annual Basis)
• Employee name • Employee number • Manager name • Job title • Assignment number • Region/location • Full- or part-time designation • Compensation program • Company start date • Position start date • Term date	• Base pay • Actual sales performance for each performance measure in the sales incentive plan (e.g., volume, profit dollars, profit margin, profit growth) • Actual incentive compensation attributable to each performance measure in the sales plan • Sales performance goals for each performance measure in the sales plan • Target incentive compensation based on performance goals for each performance measure in the sales plan • Other incentives paid (e.g., any other rewards outside the incentive plan)

the plan is aligned and functioning in sync with how revenue is actually generated. Understanding how revenue is generated and what happens on a year-over-year basis allows the organization to determine the best type of revenue to measure through the compensation plan. If the strategic plan is based on generating a specific type of revenue (e.g., new accounts), a PAR analysis provides a snapshot of actual revenue and communicates whether the plan design drives attainment of the strategic goals.

As shown in Figure 8-2, company revenue in 2008 was $385 million. The company needs to grow by 5 percent or more in 2009. Because it anticipates churn will be about 13 percent, it needs an overall growth of at least 18 percent (5 percent growth plus the 13 percent it expects to lose) to make its 2009 revenue goal of $405 million. Primarily, that growth is expected to come from penetration ($50 million, or 12 percent, of 2009 revenue). Acquisition of new accounts is expected to add $20 million, or 5 percent growth. To meet its growth goal, the company should ensure that plan measures and mechanics place a

The Six Analytics

PAR analysis: Short for "penetration revenue, acquisition revenue and retention revenue." Looks at churn (i.e., lost revenue), revenue penetration in existing accounts and new-acquisition revenue from new clients. It is used to determine "real" corporate revenue growth.

Compensation cost of sales: Looks at the cost of a compensation plan based upon revenue generated by the representatives on the plan. It looks at sales representative total compensation (base salary plus commissions/incentives) and the corresponding annualized revenue, typically for a full year.

Sales representative displacement: Examines the potential effect of the new plan on sales representative earnings. It should examine performance and earnings retrospectively and prospectively.

Pay, performance and differentiation: Examines how much representatives earn at different performance levels.

Average pay composition: Examines the composition of incentive pay (actual versus target) by each plan component and measure for sales representatives.

Performance distributions: Provides a histogram of sales representative performance for a given metric. It looks at a group of sales representatives and the percentage who achieve various performance levels.

significant focus on retention and penetration, thereby directing sales representative behavior to growing those revenue streams.

What to Look for in a PAR Analysis

Look for any significant increase or decrease in revenue over prior periods. Such fluctuation may indicate changes in representative behaviors or the market. Also, ensure the plan aligns with how revenue is generated and the strategic direction the company is charting for the future. If the plan is paying for acquisition when the majority of business comes from penetration, this may indicate a misalignment of the plan with the structure or direction of the business.

Compensation Cost of Sales

Most sales compensation consultants and corporate executives would strongly agree that the true measure of a plan's cost is total compensation dollars paid out as a percent of sales. This reveals the compensation cost of sales (CCOS), an analysis that provides insight into the compensation plan's effectiveness. (Note: Total compensation dollars can be broken out in base salary or fixed

FIGURE 8-2

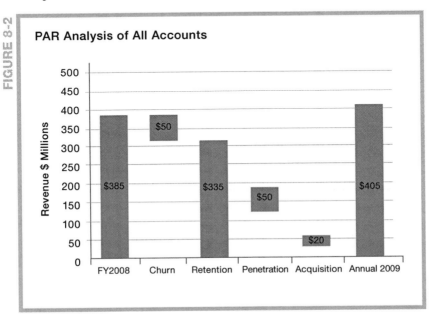

PAR Analysis of All Accounts

compensation cost of sales and commission or bonus dollars, or variable compensation cost of sales. When looking at variable pay, the amounts used need to be directly attributed to the revenue credited for particular sales.)

To calculate CCOS for any sales population, add the primary elements of compensation (base salaries and incentives) and exclude benefits, perquisites, special incentives and expenses for each person in the population. Then divide the total by the sum of all credited sales revenue generated by the same population. (Note: Typically, sales credited revenue is best defined as revenue credited to the salesforce for a particular sale. For companies with recurring revenue, annual or 12-month revenue may be used. This is to help review results with cross-industry benchmarks. Many companies with multiyear deals or recurring revenue will credit past the 12-month period, so it is important to know what type of revenue is being compared when looking across industries.)

CCOS helps a company understand what it is paying a sales population on a total cost perspective. Knowing and monitoring CCOS and conducting the proper analysis can help drive the right costs to the right area and ensure the company is paying an appropriate amount for each sale. When comparing against past plans, higher costs of sales will directly affect the bottom line. Any increase of magnitude year over year is something to watch and understand, especially if these increases are due to unexpected consequences arising from changes in plan design. (See "Tracking Compensation Cost of Sales.")

A company's CCOS may be influenced by:

- **Product margins:** High-margin businesses or products have more room and/or are more willing to use their margins to drive sales performance. This manifests as higher rates of pay or commissions. In industries with very high margins (e.g., software), the compensation costs will be much higher. Specifically, the more a company sells traditional license products (with high margins), the more it is willing to pay its salesforce.

- **Volume deal size:** Typically, high-volume or big deals (in total dollars) have lower CCOS. The reason is relatively simple: The effort to close a $20,000 deal typically is not 20 times more than it takes to close a $1,000 deal. This may also extend to multiyear deals if revenue is credited after the year (an uncommon practice). Multiyear deals typically have larger extended volume or residual annual revenue, which tends to lower CCOS if it is counted. One important point: If volume takes a seller into high commission rates or accelerators, CCOS may increase as volume increases.

- **Business maturity:** Less mature or early stage businesses tend to have a higher CCOS compared to more established businesses because growing a market is more important and strategically more significant for less mature companies. "Any sale is a good sale" may be part of the strategy because market share is very low. This philosophy typically drives companies to pay more for a sale. On the flip side, early stage or startup companies typically have less sales support (allowing dollars to be shifted to sales costs) and are more leveraged toward at-risk pay.

Tracking Compensation Cost of Sales

The best way to track CCOS — and truly know what you are paying for — is to look at its components, including:

- **Tenure:** The cost of ramping up new hires or new channels may outstrip that of experienced representatives or channels. Note that that different job roles and channels may have different ramp-up times.

- **Performance:** Breaking out CCOS by performance quartiles can lend understanding about the cost of lower-performing representatives versus higher performers. In most plans, because of fixed base salaries, lower-quartile performers can be up to three times as expensive as top-quartile performers.

- **Job roles:** Different job roles have different costs associated with them. Knowing the costs for each can help ensure the proper job resources and roles are deployed to the right opportunities. It also demonstrates the costs of adding "overlay" positions in an account.

- **Pay components:** Knowing how pay is delivered, through which pay components and the overall cost of that pay can aid decision making about which components have the biggest effect and what the effect costs the company.

- **Revenue crediting:** How an organization credits its revenue also can affect CCOS. Recurring revenue and/or multiyear contracts can create measurement complications. Traditionally, calculation of CCOS is based on 12 months of revenue. Recurring revenue that comes in after a 12-month period or from a multiyear contract that is not credited in the current year will not be factored in the revenue calculations. Revenue crediting issues come up when costs are paid up front for a sale, but revenue is not yet recognized. Some industries with very low churn (i.e., insurance, financial services) typically pay for new revenue, understanding that accounts will recur for many years to come. In some cases, companies that pay a sales representative for multiyear revenue at the time of bookings will increase CCOS in any given year, while decreasing it in future years when the revenue arrives.

- **Pay philosophy:** Pay and pay philosophy typically are tightly linked. Having a pay philosophy that states "we want to pay above market" obviously will cause CCOS to rise. Similarly, a philosophy that states "we pay at or below market" will reduce CCOS. Historically, companies tend to target certain pay levels (e.g., 60th percentile). If quota or revenue volume also is at the 60th percentile of market, the overall CCOS will be at the 60th percentile, too.

What to Look for in a CCOS Analysis

Any increases or decreases in cost based upon plan changes or behavioral changes may indicate that representatives are being overpaid or underpaid. Overpayments may suggest a flaw in the design or that representatives have found a way to beat the plan and earn more money in unintended ways. Underpayments could mean some components or targets are too difficult or unattainable.

Sales Representative Displacement

The sales representative displacement analysis looks at the different periods between prior-year and/or current-year earnings versus new or projected earnings to determine how any proposed plan changes may affect or displace sales representatives' earnings. It also measures how money flows across the population — from low performers to high performers. This is particularly important if the overall compensation cost is projected to be neutral. Analyses to perform include:

- Estimated earnings under the new plan based on "old" (i.e., current- or prior-year) performance data. This looks at the displacement or change in earnings under the new plan versus the prior or current plan.

- Estimated earnings under the old plan based on new or projected performance data. When conducted after the plan has been in place, this analysis can show how changes in behavior drive changes in incentive pay. Similar payments from one year to another, especially if the plan has changed, may suggest little behavior change. This analysis can serve as a valuable comparison to persuade or dissuade representatives of certain perceptions. For example, sales representatives may believe they are losing opportunities under a new plan and would have earned more under the old plan. Using the analysis to disprove that belief (assuming it is, in fact, incorrect) can stem turnover and heighten job satisfaction.

- (Estimated) earnings on new plan using new (or projected) performance data. This analysis looks at actual (or estimated) earnings and actual (or estimated) results.

Figure 8-3 shows the results of these three analyses and the effect of the change on the sales population.

What to Look for in a Displacement Analysis

Large swings in earnings either up or down indicate that the plan changes year over year are having an effect. If the effect is positive and was intended, then the plan is working as expected. If the effect was unintended, further analysis is necessary to determine why it is occurring and what plan adjustments are necessary.

Understanding Representative Displacement

1 Sales Reps	2 Old Plan Actual Earnings	New Plan on Old Performance Data			Old Plan on New Performance Data			New Plan on New Performance Data		
		3 Earnings	4 Change	5 Displacement Percent	6 Earnings	7 Change	8 Displacement Percent	9 Earnings	10 Change	11 Displacement Percent
Rep A	$95	$90	($5)	(5.3%)	$100	$5	5.3%	$105	$10	10.5%
Rep B	$85	$80	($5)	(5.9%)	$75	($10)	(11.8%)	$60	($25)	(29.4%)
Rep C	$100	$100	$0	–	$100	$0	–	$110	$10	10%
Rep D	$120	$130	$10	7.7%	$135	$15	12.5%	$140	$20	16.7%
Total	$400	$400	$0	0	$410	$10	2.5%	$415	$15	3.75%

Column 2 (from the left) shows individual representatives how much they earned in the prior year (e.g., 2008). Column 3 shows what a representative would earn under the new plan for maintaining 2008 results. This does not account for any change in behavior that may occur. Columns 4 and 5 show the displacement (difference in earnings) and the percent change when compared to Column 2 (2008 earnings). The sum of these columns is the total displacement and percent change at an aggregate level. The change in this example is zero, indicating the new designs are not intended to be cost-neutral. (Note: This does not take into account behavioral changes from plan designs, and new strategic direction will

cause representatives to affect the plan. It is a comparison that holds past years' performance constant to determine potential costs.)

Columns 6 through 8 show how representatives would fare under the 2008 plan if they performed at 2009 projected levels, and then compares earnings to 2008 (Column 2). Columns 9 through 11 compare 2009 earnings from 2009 projected results to 2008 earnings. Once this plan is in place, these analyses also can be performed with actual data, perhaps running quarterly comparisons.

FIGURE 8-3

Pay, Performance and Differentiation

This calculation looks at how much representatives earn at different performance levels. This set of analytics helps answer several questions:

- Are the top earners also the top performers? Are the bottom earners the worst performers?
- How are the top-earning representatives getting those high incentive payments (i.e., through right or wrong behaviors)?
- Are the lowest earners the lowest performers?
- Do the high performers earn substantially more than the low performers?

The overall goal is to verify that pay and performance are both differentiated and aligned for the representative populations. Poor pay-for-performance alignment and differentiation often lead to higher cost of sales because low-performing representatives are paid too much relative to their results. It can cause top-performing representatives to leave the company if they feel they are not receiving rewards commensurate with their efforts. The charts in Figure 8-4 show typical pay and performance correlations.

Figure 8-5 shows the differentiation between the lower performers versus higher performers by performance measure (Measure 1 and Measure 2). The graph shows earnings in each performance percentile (from the 10th percentile to the 90th percentile) as a percent of median. Look for differentiation, such as a representative who performs at the 90th percentile for Measure 1 earns 200 percent more than a median performer. This is a good differentiation. Conversely, on Measure 2 the 90th-percentile performer earns 50 percent more than the median performer. The company must decide whether that is enough differentiation for that measure. Also, it appears that Measure 2 is weighted more heavily than Measure 1. As a result, overall incentive earnings are being pulled down. Perhaps there's not enough differentiation for top performers.

FIGURE 8-4

Typical Pay and Performance Correlations

Chart 1: Tight Relationship

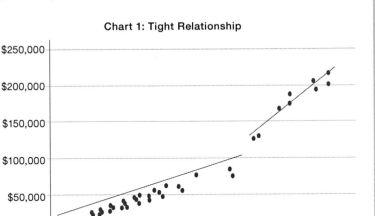

Chart 1 shows a tight relationship between pay and performance where sales representative pay is aligned with performance.

Chart 2: Outliers

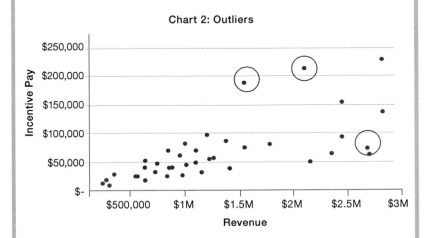

Chart 2 shows a poor relationship, in that some top performers are earning less than or the same as lower performers.

FIGURE 8-4

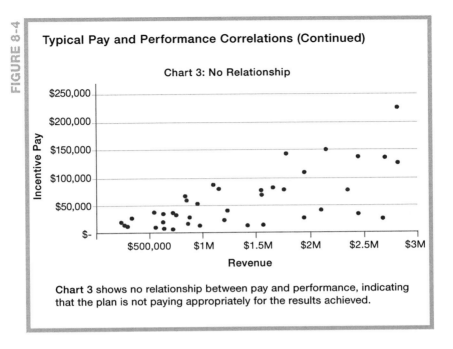

Typical Pay and Performance Correlations (Continued)

Chart 3: No Relationship

Chart 3 shows no relationship between pay and performance, indicating that the plan is not paying appropriately for the results achieved.

What to Look for in a Differentiation Analysis

Look for misalignment between top performers and top earners. If lower performers are earning more than top performers, there is an issue with the plan. Additionally, if the differentiation is not sufficiently significant between median and top performers, representatives may not be motivated to achieve higher results.

Average Pay Composition

This analytic looks at the composition of incentive pay by plan component (or measure) for sales representatives. It shows how sales representatives are earning incentive dollars and through which measures. It allows the company to determine whether actual payouts are in line with the target pay envisioned when the plan was designed.

As shown in Figure 8-6, if actual payouts or the percent earned per measure are out of line with the targets for each measure, something is occurring to shift the plan away from what was envisioned. This analytic helps isolate the problem and allows a deeper dive into potential causes; adjustments can then be made as appropriate.

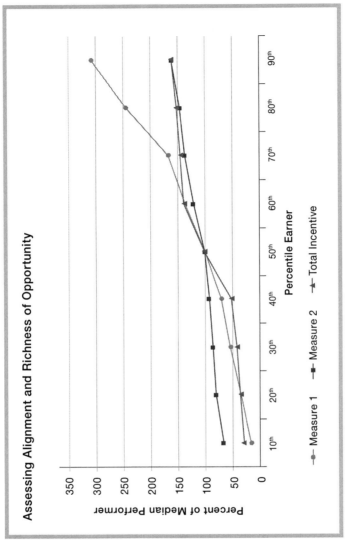

Assessing Alignment and Richness of Opportunity

Percent of Median Performer

Percentile Earner

—◆— Measure 1   —■— Measure 2   —▲— Total Incentive

FIGURE 8-5

FIGURE 8-6

Pay Composition by Compensation Element

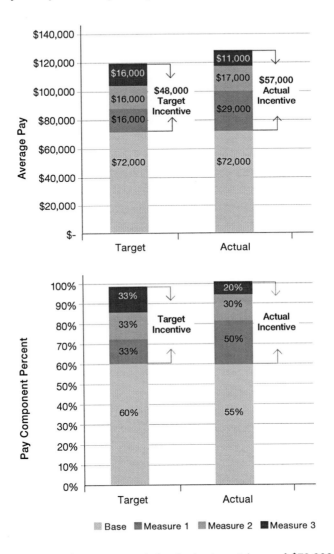

In this example, a representative had a target base of $72,000 and an incentive of $48,000 for an overall 60/40 mix. The plan has three measures, with each having a weighting of 33 percent, or 16 percent of the $48,000 target incentive. Overall, from a TTC perspective, this equates to 13 percent of total pay for each measure. This representative earned $29,000 for Measure 1 versus the targeted $16,000. Additionally, the representative earned well below the expectation on Measure 3 ($11,000). Measure 2 appears to be close to target.

What does this analysis say about the plan? It was designed to have a 60/40 mix; actual mix is 55/45, with the incentive target split 50 percent for Measure 1, 30 percent for Measure 2 and 20 percent for Measure 3. Does this actual mix create an issue for the compensation philosophy and overall strategy? Additionally, the problem seems to lie with Measure 1, as earnings were more than double the target. Is this coming at the expense of Measure 3, which appears to be ignored? Has the representative found greater opportunity than expected? Is there really less opportunity for Measure 3, or is there gaming of the plan or some other reason for actual payments to be so far off? The analysis provides something tangible about results and plan performance. The next step is figuring out what is causing the difference and what, if anything, needs to be done.

What to Look for in an Average Pay Composition Analysis
Look for differences in earnings, weighting or mix between the actual results and plan targets and projections. This provides an idea of what is really happening with the plan and suggests areas to probe to determine the cause of the variations.

Performance Distributions

A performance distribution is a histogram of sales representative performance for a given metric. It analyzes the performance of a group of sales representatives, isolating the percentages of representatives at various performance levels. This analytic helps determine how many representatives are above, at or below target, providing a view into the effectiveness of targets or quotas. If too many representatives are below quota, perhaps targets are too high. If too many are above quota, targets may be too low. This analytic connects quota-setting to payouts. Because quotas are so tightly aligned to pay, it is necessary to understand the performance distribution among representatives. You can design the best plan in the world … but if you have the wrong quotas or targets, the plan will appear broken.

Typically, 60 percent to 65 percent of sales representatives should be at or above target for a measure or the overall plan. Ten percent should be at or above the excellence point, and 10 percent should fall below threshold. This distribution creates a bell curve. If actual distribution is off from this target, it usually indicates some sort of issue with the plan, quota or measure. Figures 8-7, 8-8, 8-9 and 8-10 should look familiar, as they were in the Chapter 6 quota quiz. They show various performance distributions and provide a valuable snapshot of how a plan is working.

- **Poor goal-setting, effective allocation:** In Figure 8-7, the company missed its goal, although sales representative performance is well-distributed. This may indicate quotas were too high for the majority of sales representatives.

- **Market variations or performance penalties:** In Figure 8-8, a disproportionate number of representatives are above and below quota. This may indicate that the quotas did not take into account different market opportunities in representatives' territories. Some territories may have greater opportunity than others, but if quotas are set equally across all markets, it can create earnings disparities.

- **Effective goal-setting, poor allocation:** In Figure 8-9, the company exceeded goal, which appears to have been set accurately based upon the overall distribution of representatives above and below goal. The problem appears to be that the quotas were not allocated to representatives appropriately; many of the representatives performing above quota likely had quotas that were too low, while some who failed to meet quota probably had quotas that were too high.

- **Effective goal-setting and allocation:** Figure 8-10 is a great distribution. The representatives are tightly distributed around quota. This indicates that the plan is effective and spurring the right results.

What to Look for in Performance Distributions
Uneven distribution of representatives below or above quota, or too many representatives bunched in different percentiles, may

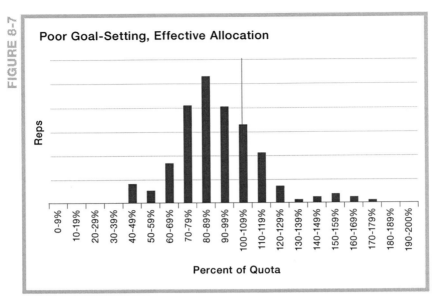

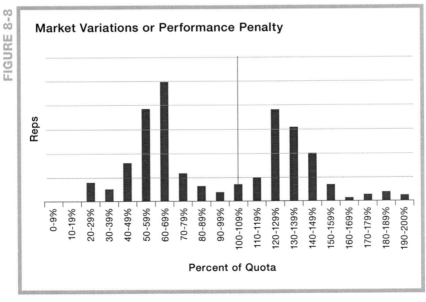

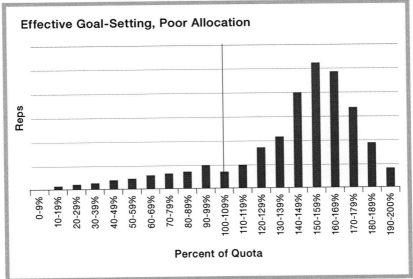

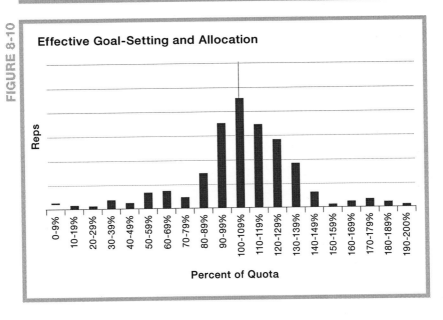

mean the quota-setting process is not aligned with the market opportunity.

When Are Midyear Adjustments Warranted?

Midyear adjustments should be considered only under the following circumstances:

- CCOS is significantly over budget.

- Top performers are earning less than they have in previous years and do not have enough differentiation from low performers.

- Too few representatives are on pace to make the target compensation levels.

Using the six analytics allows a company to identify a plan's assets and deficits. Performing the analyses prior to rollout will reveal necessary adjustments, if any, to the new plan design. Once a plan is operational, the analyses will tell whether the plan is functioning as expected. In the end, the evaluation needs to provide just enough information, just in time. Analytics will produce the best results when you remember:

- Pull the right amount of detail from the right systems.
- Don't overload the user with complex analytics.
- Ensure the plan provides the means to execute the strategy.

Conclusion

Now you have a complete look at how sales compensation plans should be designed, assessed and implemented. Stepping back from the entire process, you can understand how each step leads to the next and how the steps are interdependent. I'm sure you see how critical a role strategy plays in the entire equation, and you can better understand why a plan that is not based in strategy is doomed to fail.

You also have charts and practices that can be used to debate and grapple with the key aspects of sales incentive design. By applying these concepts and analyses in your review of any sales plan, there should be few questions or issues that you will be unable to explain. These practices provide the science of sales compensation; the art comes with experience and understanding your organization and its strategy, corporate culture, products and markets, and sales team. The key is to blend the science and art in a way that creates success.

I sincerely hope this book gives you an education commensurate with what my clients and colleagues have provided me throughout my career. I believe that the more we share, the more we learn. I wish you the very best with all of your sales compensation challenges.

Appendix

Determining a Compensation Philosophy

Assess where your company falls on the spectrum.

Role of Pay

Pay Highly Prominent   Pay Less Prominent

Pay is a significant, prominent driver in the employee value proposition

Performance Criteria

Individual Measures   Enterprisewide Measures

Primarily line-of-sight measures with some enterprisewide financial measures

Internal/External Value

Internal Equity   External Competitiveness

To facilitate recruiting work, valuation weighted toward the external market

Competitive Positioning

Less Competitive   Highly Competitive

Compensation programs designed to give high upside potential
for high performance

Mix of Pay

Highly Fixed   Highly Variable

Significant portion of employees' pay at risk or variable to drive performance

Governance and Decision-Making

Decentralized Governance   Centralized Governance

Global compensation framework and governance,
with some local market flexibility

Communication

Open Communications   Selective Communications

Relatively open communications are thought to support
a pay-for-performance culture

Example: Sales Compensation Philosophy

Principles	Stated Philosophy
1. Key business strategy	• Increase new revenue by acquisition of new customers. • Retain current customers at the 95-percent level. • Move into untapped markets. • Sell more strategic products.
2. Preferred performance measures	• New business revenue • Margin dollars • Retention revenue • Total revenue
3. Basis of measurement; individual versus team	• Performance will be measured at the individual level on all measures.
4. Eligibility requirements	• Reps must meet minimum thresholds to be eligible to earn incentives.
5. Competitive positioning; targeting pay versus market	• We will pay at the 50th percentile of the market for on-target performance.
6. Desired dispersion of pay across performance range	• Top performers (90th percentile) will earn pay that is three times the target incentive.
7. Degree of uniformity in incentive plan design	• Plan mechanics will be consistent across the regions, although performance measures and their relative weight, as well as individual goals, may vary based on strategic objectives of each job.
8. Goals versus quotas	• Goals will be set at the national level.
9. Formulaic versus discretionary plans	• Plans will be formulaic with no managerial discretion to adjust payouts, except in the instance of large transfers of accounts.
10. Cash versus non-cash incentives	• In addition to cash incentives we will run two contests per year in certain markets emphasizing specific products or other sales objectives.
11. Caps and upside earnings	• Earnings will not be capped, however, the company reserves the right to limit earnings on transfers of business.
12. Plan governance and administration	• Day-to-day plan administration will be managed by the sales operations team, made up of sales, finance, and HR professionals • Annual plan audits will conducted by sales operations and reviewed by sales management, finance and HR.

Interview Guide: General Management

We are here today to discuss your role and to build our fact base in the first stage of our project looking at the organization's sales effectiveness. In the next few weeks, we will interview several senior individuals like you. Generally, we will ask questions about how you see the organization currently and your vision for the future. To help make that vision a reality, we also will discuss how we can improve the structure and motivation of the sales organization.

The data collected from these interviews will be compiled, analyzed and presented in aggregate. No comments or specific responses will be attributed to any individual directly. The success of this project depends on your honest and thoughtful responses, so please take your time and be as frank as possible. We expect to take approximately one hour of your time. If you have any questions now or during our conversation, please feel free to jump in.

Background
1. Tell us about your background, both inside and outside the company.
2. Describe your current role. What are your main responsibilities? What is the scope of your responsibility?
3. What are the critical success factors for your role?
4. What interactions do you have with other functions or levels in the organization?

Strategy
1. How do your objectives fit within the larger company goals?
2. How do company goals and strategies cascade throughout the organization?
3. Where do you see your organization heading? What will need to change to accomplish future goals and successfully support revenue growth?

Sales Administration

1. Describe how accounts are assigned to the sales representatives. How frequently are these assignments reviewed?
2. Describe how quotas are assigned to the sales representatives.
3. What are the key challenges that you encounter (in your function and/or role) as the sales compensation plans are administered?
4. What personnel, technical or process issues are you aware of?
5. How often are errors made? Do you have defined processes for correcting them?
6. What are the most important factors in improving process flow (speed, quality, flexibility, cost, etc.)?

Driving Performance

1. How accurate is the data derived to assess performance? Which factors affect this accuracy?
2. What are the key performance indicators used to measure sales achievement? How often are these reviewed?
3. What are the key managerial actions that are taken as a result of these performance indicators?
4. Describe the incentive compensation programs. What are their strengths and weaknesses?
5. Is the company able to use the incentive compensation programs to attract, motivate and retain the right talent? Describe the evidence that supports your answer.
6. Do the plans drive the correct behavior? How?
7. Are costs in line with appropriate budgets? What are the biggest cost drivers?

About the Author

Joseph F. DiMisa is a Senior Vice President and leader of the salesforce effectiveness practice for Sibson Consulting, the strategic HR consulting division of The Segal Co. He works with leading companies to develop sales strategies and effectiveness programs that drive profitable growth. DiMisa has more than 15 years' experience in the corporate and professional consulting world, providing thought leadership and expertise to both large and small organizations. His areas of responsibility include direct sales planning and management, sales segmentation/targeting, sales compensation, quota-setting, sales channel management and strategic planning.

DiMisa is the author of *The Fisherman's Guide to Selling: Reeling in the Sale — Hook, Line and Sinker* (Adams Media, 2007) and is a frequent guest writer for many well-known business publications. He is an accomplished speaker and industry expert on all salesforce planning and effectiveness topics. DiMisa is a certified WorldatWork sales compensation instructor and is involved in designing the association's sales compensation program content and training curriculum.